THE WORLD OF HOSPICE
SPIRITUAL CARE

A Practical Guide for Palliative Care Chaplains

Dr. Douglas G. Sullivan

ISBN 978-1-64028-765-5 (Paperback)
ISBN 978-1-64028-766-2 (Digital)

Christian Faith Publishing, Inc.
296 Chestnut Street
Meadville, PA 16335
www.christianfaithpublishing.com

Printed in the United States of America

ACKNOWLEDGEMENT

For my dear wife, Debbie:
You have always been my best cheerleader, constant companion, and forever-friend. Just as we promised each other some thirty-five years ago, I will love you always and forever for your never-ending love and faithful support. Thank you for your always practical words of wisdom, your desire to walk with me through times of uncertain change, and your continuous support of my God-given dreams. You are an incredible partner in the journey to which God has called us.

Finally, thanks to Jesus Christ, who set the example for me to become the Word of God incarnate to my culture and live out His glory—full of grace and truth.

CONTENTS

INTRODUCTION

Chaplains serve in interdisciplinary teams to help relieve pain and suffering and to improve patients' quality of life. One area of chaplaincy, serving patients and families in a hospice situation, requires members of hospice teams to have specialized knowledge in their area of expertise. At the same time, hospice chaplains must be familiar with other areas of hospice work and their functions, because hospice care components interrelate. Working in the hospice environment offers tremendous satisfaction and challenges. This book addresses those challenges and prepares chaplains to allow God's presence to shine through them as they minister effectively in palliative care[1] outreaches.

---

[1] The NHPCO defines palliative care as "patient and family-centered care that optimizes quality of life by anticipating, preventing, and treating suffering. Palliative care throughout the continuum of illness involves addressing physical, intellectual, emotional, social, and spiritual needs and to facilitate patient autonomy, access to information and choice."

This work explores the world of hospice and hospice spiritual care. In the first section, this practical guide examines hospice movement history, philosophy and concepts of care, program models, and interdisciplinary teams. Section two discusses the psychosocial and spiritual aspects of pain; spiritual assessments and spiritual care plans; the role of spiritual care staff; grief, bereavement, and mourning; and staff grief and stress management.

A thorough analysis of these topics introduces individuals to the world of hospice, which helps the critical role of the spiritual counselor (hospice chaplain) to emerge. Thus, a better understanding of these concepts and the resulting increased technical competence allows hospice chaplains more freedom to impact patients', families', and caregivers' lives through the transforming presence of God's incarnational glory.

THE WORLD OF HOSPICE

Introduction

Hospice workers must determine how they can prepare to work with the dying and learn more about their essential positions. According to Dame Cicely Saunders, "You learn the care of the dying from the dying themselves. But only if you look at them with respect and never merely with pity, and allow them to teach you. It is they who show us the fear of death is overcome."[2] The call to work with the dying is a call to work with patients in a sacred place—the place of their dying. It is a place where masks fall away as people stand on the doorstep of the unknown, letting go of everything familiar and learning to trust what is to come. As patients learn to let go, so do chaplains. Ministers must let go of previously-held notions about death and allow

---

[2] Dame Cicely Saunders, "The Moment of Truth: Care of the Dying Patient," in *Death and Dying: Current Issues in Treatment of the Dying Person*, ed. Leonard Pearson (Cleveland, OH: Press of Case Western Reserve University, 1969), 78.

new insights and awareness to grow in the midst of their ignorance. They also must discard the need to always be the teachers and become the students.

Hospice chaplains must also possess a thorough knowledge of techniques, pain, and symptom control, as well as an understanding of the concepts of hospice care, the process of death and dying, the concepts of grief and bereavement, and working in interdisciplinary teams. In order to provide the most current knowledge, as well as excellent skills in assessment and intervention, quality hospice care depends on highly skilled hospice staff. This section provides basic information about hospice care to chaplains who are members of interdisciplinary teams, and it also addresses challenges chaplains encounter as they effectively minister in the world of hospice.

HOSPICE MOVEMENT HISTORY

Hospice care is both an ancient philosophy and a modern health care concept. It is as old as way stations set up by religious orders to nurture and restore weary travelers and as new as the most technologically and pharmacologically sophisticated methods of managing pain. The modern-day concept of hospice as a place to care for the dying finds its basis in two hospices opened by the Irish Sisters of Charity in the late nineteenth century: Our Lady's Hospice in Dublin and St. Joseph's in London opened to care only for the dying, which was a radical approach for the time.[3]

---

[3] Florence S. Wald discusses the development of hospice care in two articles. See Florence S. Wald, "Hospice Care Concepts," *Hospice Education Program for Nurses,* U.S. Department of Health and Human Services Publication No. HRA 81-27, 1981, 5-19. See also Florence S. Wald, Zelda Foster and Henry J. Wald, "The Hospice Movement as a Health Care Reform," *American Journal of Nursing* 79, no. 10 (October 1979).

Dame Cicely Saunders

The modern idea of hospice as a place emphasizing loving care for those who are dying, as well as the best possible place to control pain began with Dr. Cicely Saunders. Saunders developed the concept of hospice care, founding St. Christopher's Hospice in 1967. First trained as a nurse and later as a social worker, Saunders felt distraught over the suffering of dying hospital patients. She began to dream with one of her patients, David, about building a place to serve as a combination of a hospital and a home. This would be a place that would not only care for the medical needs of the dying but also for their spiritual and emotional needs. When David, a refugee from the Warsaw Ghetto, died, he left Saunders the equivalent of one thousand dollars, saying, "I want to be a window in your new home."[4]

Realizing she needed to learn more to fulfill this dream, Saunders completed her training as a physician and began working at St. Joseph's Hospice in 1958. After nearly a decade of planning and observation, she opened St. Christopher's Hospice in 1967. The sixty-two-bed hospice inpatient facility was located in London, England. It was

---

[4] Sandol Stoddard, *The Hospice Movement: A Better Way of Caring for the Dying* (New York: Stein and Day Publishers, 1978), 30, 97.

the first facility of its kind to use meticulous assessments of patients' physical and psychological problems to diagnose pain. Under Saunders' leadership, an interdisciplinary team provided psychosocial support and medication. Most patients improved and remained alert and symptom-free until death.

Saunders recognized the importance of including family members in hospice care, and she encouraged them to take active roles to care for their loved ones. Her team provided family support and assistance during, and even after, patients' illnesses. Saunders also grasped the significance of physical environments on emotional and physical health. She designed St. Christopher's as a window-filled home of security, comfort, and peace.[5]

As her work with hospice continued, Saunders emphasized three important components of hospice care: superb patient care with emphasis on the relief of all types of pain (physical, emotional, spiritual, and social), research, and education. Saunders defined the principles and essential elements of terminal care, and she believed caregivers could interpret them in different ways to meet the needs of different locations. Providing excellent care was the import-

---

[5] Nancy Burns, Kim Carney, and Bob Brobst, "Hospice: A Design for Home Care for the Terminally Ill," *Holistic Nursing Practice* 3, no. 2 (February 1989): 65-76.

ant factor, not the location the care was given or the organizational structure of the hospice program. When first describing the nature of hospice care, Saunders developed lists of the elements and principles upon which all caregivers should base hospice care.[6]

Elisabeth Kübler-Ross

As news about Saunders' work with the dying reached North America, Elisabeth Kübler-Ross, a Swedish born psychiatrist, began her work with terminally ill patients at the University of Chicago Medical School. Originally, people considered her methods, such as interviewing dying patients, very unorthodox, almost costing Kübler-Ross her career. Her research in the areas of death and dying eventually led to her book, *On Death and Dying*, which quickly became a bestseller. Kübler-Ross asserted that Western culture's widespread denial of death and the isolation and conspiracy of silence that surrounds the terminally ill is extremely unhealthy. She also described five ways to cope

---

[6] Dame Cicely Saunders, *The Management of Terminal Disease* (London: Edward Arnold, Ltd., 1978), 195-202.

with approaching death. Her stages also apply to bereaved family members going through the process of grief.[7]

Despite many differences in their approaches, Kübler-Ross and Saunders focused on the needs of the dying and the importance of allowing terminally ill patients to tell caregivers what they really need. Finally, both of these pioneers understood the benefits of an interdisciplinary approach and the need for caregivers to also care for themselves.

Hospice Program Growth

Until the 1900s, family members cared for most patients, even the critically injured or ill, at home. Doctors made house calls, and if death appeared imminent, they helped the families prepare for the approaching tragic event. Patients usually died at home where people could say goodbye and spend precious last moments together. Death was a part of people's lives. Following WWII, health care in the United States experienced a time of phenomenal development and increased technological advances. Incredible achievements, both in curative and rehabilitative care, contributed to depersonalizing of care, especially for the terminally ill.

---

[7] Elisabeth Kübler-Ross, *On Death and Dying* (New York: Macmillian Publishing Company, 1969), 51, 63, 93, 97, 123.

The beginning of antibiotics, improved surgical techniques, and impressive advances in technology brought about almost miraculous cures. However, such amazing progress came with a steep price. The provision of medical care shifted from homes to efficient hospitals, impersonal environments where family members were in the way and doctors based diagnoses on laboratory results rather than clinical judgment. With all of these new miracles of treatment, the personal side of medical care for patients and families often disappeared. For those doctors could cure, the new health care system offered impersonal, but very effective help. But for many who were dying, it gave very little hope or comfort. Caregivers often pushed aside and isolated terminally ill patients and their families. Silence descended to cover up death, which people often saw as a healthcare system failure. Eventually, patients and their families, dissatisfied at this development, began demanding more humane treatment. Many desired inclusion in decision making, information about what was taking place, and treatment as if they really mattered. In this climate of discontent, news about Saunders and Kübler-Ross spread rapidly across the United States.[8]

---

[8] Wald, "Hospice Care Concepts," 11-15.

While visiting the United States as a guest lecturer at Yale University in 1968, Saunders assisted to establish viable hospice programs in North America. They eventually started three programs: one at Royal Victoria Hospital in Montreal, one at St. Luke's Hospital in New York, and one at the newly-founded Connecticut Hospice in New Haven in 1974. Since then, the number of hospice programs in the United States has grown extensively. Hospice continued to grow with the creation of the National Hospice Organization in 1978. This organization created educational conferences and published directories of hospice care providers.[9] The National Hospice Organization existed until February 2000 when it was renamed the National Hospice and Palliative Care Organization.[10]

In 1991, more than one thousand eight hundred hospices were in operation. As of 2011, there were over five thousand three hundred hospice programs in the United States alone.[11] Some experts claim hospice represents one

---

[9] Kelly Noe, Pamela Smith, and Mustafa Younis, "Calls for Reform to the U.S. Hospice System," *Ageing International* 37, no. 2 (June 2012): 230.

[10] "About NHPCO," National Hospice and Palliative Care Organization, accessed March 20, 2015, http://www.nhpco.org/about-nhpco.

[11] Noe, 230.

of the fastest growing medical and social movements in the United States. Several factors contributed to this rapid increase in hospice programs, including community outrage, cost, cultural emphasis on autonomy, and governmental and industry support.

Community Outrage: Enraged by perceptions of isolation, lack of support among the medical and nursing communities, exclusion from the decision-making process, and the unnecessary suffering of dying family members, people not only became disenchanted with the lack of quality of terminal care provided by the healthcare system, they strongly felt that something could be done to change this unacceptable climate. Out of their tremendous need, men and women banded together to establish new hospice programs for their local communities. Until recently though, hospice program staff were still viewed by many health care professionals as radical outsiders who were forcing unwanted changes in the system they were content to be a part of.

Cost: Most analysts who study the costs of health care agree that a large percentage of our nation's health care dollars are spent on futile and ineffective treatments that only prolong the dying process. Since effective and high quality palliative care does not usually require costly, invasive diagnostic procedures or treatment, hospice care is usually much less expensive than traditional curative measures. The hospice emphasis on home care and using volunteers also contributes to containing the cost of providing for the terminally ill.

Cultural Emphasis on Autonomy: Throughout the twentieth century, the U.S. experienced a huge surge of interest in personal autonomy. This resulted in new emphasis on the rights of patients and their families to be included in health care decisions. In the health care environment, autonomy is defined as the right of patients and their families to be included in health care decisions, to be informed of all possible options, and to accept or reject treatments or procedures. Hospice bases its care on patient/family autonomy.

Governmental and Industry Support: In 1983, Congress extended Medicare coverage to include hospice care, and many states now also offer a Medicaid Hospice Benefit as well. Governmental support of hospice care has ensured the financial stability of most Medicare-certified hospice programs. In addition, many private insurance companies also recognize the cost-effectiveness of hospice care and cover hospice services as a part of their package of benefits. Now, having examined key figures and events that caused the hospice movement to grow in Western culture, this writing will next discuss hospice philosophy and concepts of care.

HOSPICE PHILOSOPHY AND
CONCEPTS OF CARE

Hospice is based on a philosophy that embraces death as a natural part of the cycle of life. State-of-the-art control of pain and other uncomfortable symptoms, as well as the ability to address the psychosocial issues causing distress for patients and their families, support the patients' desire to die with dignity and with as much control as possible. The hospice philosophy of care is very simple: terminally ill patients deserve the best possible palliative care, and both patients and families deserve the best possible supportive care to relieve physical, emotional, spiritual, and social pain and suffering.

Philosophy of care has been an important issue for over two decades. The National Hospice Organization[12]

---

[12] The National Hospice and Palliative Care Organization (NHPCO) originally founded in 1978 as the National Hospice Organization (NHO) advocating for the needs of people facing life-limiting illness. The organization changed its name to NHPCO in February

(NHO)'s Standards of a Hospice Program of Care (1993)[13] embraced this concept. It emphasized that hospice provides support and care for persons in the last phases of incurable disease so they may live as fully and comfortably as possible. Hospice recognizes dying as a part of the normal process of living and focuses on maintaining the quality of individuals' remaining lives. Hospice affirms life, neither hastening nor postponing death. It exists in the hope and belief that through appropriate care, as well as the promotion of a caring community sensitive to their needs, patients and their families may attain a degree of mental and spiritual preparation for death that is satisfactory to them. Hospice offers palliative care to all terminally ill people and their families without regard for diagnosis, gender, sexual orientation, race, creed, disability, age, place of residence, or ability to pay.

2000. Today, NHPCO is the world's largest and most innovative national membership organization devoted exclusively to promoting access to hospice and palliative care and to maintaining quality care for persons facing the end of life and their families. See www.nhpco.org/about-nhpco for more information about the history and mission of the NHPCO.

[13] National Hospice Organization, *Standards of a Hospice Program of Care,* (Arlington, VA: NHO, 1993).

More recently, the NHPCO's Standards of Practice for Hospice Programs (2010)[14] emphasizes that hospice provides twenty-four hour palliative care to terminally ill patients in both home and inpatient settings, as well as supportive services to patients, their families, and significant others. Medically-directed interdisciplinary teams consisting of patients, families, professionals, and volunteers provide physical, social, spiritual, and emotional care during the last stages of illness, through the dying process, and during bereavement.

The NHPCO defines palliative care as the following:

> Palliative care is patient and family-centered care that optimizes quality of life by anticipating, preventing, and treating suffering. Palliative care throughout the continuum of illness involves addressing physical, intellectual, emotional, social, and spiritual needs and to facilitate patient autonomy, access to information and choice. The following features characterize palliative care philosophy and

---

[14] "Standards of Practice for Hospice Programs (2010)," National Hospice and Palliative Care Organization (NHPCO), accessed May 9, 2014, http://www.nhpco.org/standards.

delivery: care is provided and services are coordinated by an interdisciplinary team; patients, families, palliative and non-palliative heath care providers collaborate and communicate about care needs; services are available concurrently with or independent of curative or life-prolonging care; and patient and family hopes for peace and dignity are supported throughout the course of illness, during the dying process, and after death.[15]

These concepts form the foundation of palliative care and serve as the basis for hospice care. Although these concepts are separate, in actual practice, they are inseparable. The concepts are interdependent parts that form the whole of hospice care when woven together. Chaplains must integrate these concepts of care into all parts of their lives. Integrating these practices helps ministers become more authentic in their relationships with their patients. The following sections briefly examine these concepts.

_____

[15] "An Explanation of Palliative Care," National Hospice and Palliative Care Organization, accessed March 20, 2015, http://www.nhpco.org/palliative-care-0.

Emphasis of Patient and Family Autonomy

Hospice programs recognize patient and family autonomy, or self-governance, by encouraging patients and family members to take active roles in defining the goals of care and participating in all decision making. Douglas MacDonald notes that the principle of autonomy in the hospice setting means patients and family members have the right not only to refuse a particular course of treatment but also to modify treatment to meet other needs they might experience, such as the need for privacy, mental alertness, or care in particular settings or at specific times.[16]

By its very nature, hospice requires chaplains to relinquish control to the patients and families, who are the experts on how they feel and what they want. Sidney Wanzer states the goal of team care must be care that meets patient and family needs for self-governance. He argues,

> ... at present, advanced directives do not exert enough influence on either the patient's ability to control medical decision-making at the end of life or the phy-

---

[16] Douglas MacDonald, "Hospice, Entropy, and the 1990s: Toward a Hospice World View," *The American Journal of Hospice and Palliative Care* 7, no. 4. (July/August 1990): 39-47.

sician's behavior with respect to such issues in hospitals, emergency rooms, and nursing homes. There remains a considerable gap between the acceptance of the directive and its implementation. All too frequently, physicians are reluctant to withdraw aggressive treatment from hopelessly ill patients, despite clear legal precedent.[17]

Staff members, both those new to hospice care and those with years of experience, are frequently challenged by the patient's/family's expanded role in making treatment decisions. Relinquishing control can be difficult, particularly when we have been trained to be the professional in charge, always in control and performing as the teacher and helper, rather than the one who is taught and helped.

Patient and Family are the Unit of Care

Patients belong to family systems that need support during times of crisis, particularly crises involving the death of family members. Since patients and families are such

---

[17] Sidney Wanzer et al., "The Physicians Responsibility Toward Hopelessly Ill Patients: A Second Look," *The New England Journal of Medicine* 320 (March 30, 1989): 846.

interdependent parts of the system, terminal illness affects not only the patients themselves but also every other member of the family systems. All people need support as they learn to redefine their roles, adjust to loss, examine family issues, address spiritual concerns and financial matters, and determine how best to care for those who are dying. After death occurs, family members often need ongoing support and care during times of bereavement.

When providing care, chaplains need to remember that hospice defines the word *family* in broad enough terms to include relatives, close friends, lovers, and others vitally important in patients' lives. The National Hospice and Palliative Care Organization defines family as "a group of two or more individuals related by ties of blood, legal status, or affection who consider themselves a family."[18]

In many other health care organizations, the patient is the unit of care and family members are tolerated only when necessary. Patients and family members often need one another on such a deep level that severing those connections during the dying process interferes with quality of life and any opportunity for emotional healing. Hospice

---

[18] National Hospice and Palliative Care Organization, *Standards of Practice for Hospice Programs (2010)*, (Arlington, VA: NHPCO, 2010), 213.

recognizes these interconnections and works to enhance them on a deep and meaningful level.

Hospice Care is Palliative with Emphasis on Pain Control

Hospice care is palliative, rather than curative. Comfort care involves changes in treatment goals from curing patients' underlying diseases to providing comfort and relief from distressing symptoms.[19] Palliative care emphasizes management of symptoms, with special attention given to controlling pain, so hospice requires its medical staff to become specialists highly skilled in the control of pain and other symptoms. Quality of life demands that they adequately control physical symptoms. This allows patients to devote their energies to other important issues, such as reconciliation and spiritual concerns.

Death is a Natural Part of the Cycle of Life

Hospice neither hastens nor postpones death, but it accepts death as the last phase of life, just as conception and birth are the beginning phases. When cures are no lon-

---

[19] "An Explanation of Palliative Care," National Hospice and Palliative Care Organization, accessed September 9, 2013, http://www.nhpco.org/palliative-care-0.

ger realistic, teams work together to ensure that the dying process is as satisfying and fulfilling as possible so patients can experience peaceful and appropriate deaths. Instead of letting the fears of uncontrolled pain or loss of control rush people into ending life prematurely or prolonging life as long as possible regardless of its quality, the acknowledgment of death as part of the cycle of life allows them to accept life's natural ending. Stephen Levine states it this way: "To let go of the last moment and open to the next is to die consciously moment to moment."[20]

Traditionally, a patient's death was viewed as a failure on the part of the medical profession. Since cure was the only acceptable outcome, death was forbidden to enter the halls of the hospital or nursing home. If a patient persisted in dying, he/she was isolated and ignored and the call lights went unanswered for as long as possible. None of the staff wanted to be reminded that death could defeat all the latest medical technology. However, in hospice care, a death with dignity, sometimes referred to as an "appropriate" or "good" death, is seen not as a failure but as a successful completion of the cycle of life.

---

[20] Stephen Levine, *Who Dies? An Investigation of Conscious Living and Conscious Dying* (New York: Random House, Inc., 1982), 249.

Hospice Care is Holistic, Emphasizing Quality of Life

Hospice care emerges from the principle of holism—the understanding that anything that deeply affects one aspect of a person's being affects all other parts of that person's being. As people learn more about the complex interconnections that make up their lives, they develop greater appreciation for how their physical, emotional, social, and spiritual lives interweave. MacDonald summarizes:

> ... hospice's holistic paradigm helps to break false linkages between loss of independent, physical functioning and loss of dignity. Hospice focuses on the individual's uniqueness, the multiple aspects of personal identity—spanning past and present—that transcend disease and disability. Not only does hospice actively affirm the right of the severely ill to be treated as whole persons, but in so doing hospice opens a healing dialogue between those in need (who have much to teach) and the

rest of society (who have a great deal to relearn about what it is to be human).[21]

More traditional components of health care focus care on one aspect of patients: the physical body. When a cure is the most likely outcome, such emphasis on the physical is more appropriate; however, most health care professionals understand that holistic care hastens and improves healing for all their patients. In hospice care, when a cure is no longer likely, expanding caring to include the entire person is vital.

Hospice Care is Interdisciplinary

Hospice provides comprehensive care, so a team of highly trained, compassionate professionals from several different disciplines are needed to meet the patients' and families' physical, emotional, spiritual, and social needs.[22] Physicians, nurses, social workers, clergy, home health aides, pharmacists, physical and occupational therapists, and others work together to ensure they meet the needs

---

[21] Douglas MacDonald, "The Hospice World View: Healing vs. Recovery," *The American Journal of Hospice and Palliative Care* 7, no. 5 (September/October 1990): 41.

[22] National Hospice and Palliative Care Organization, *Standards of Practice for Hospice Programs (2010)*.

of the patients, families, and caregivers as completely as possible.

Traditionally, medical providers usually focused on just one aspect of patient needs. When professionals concern themselves with only one aspect of the patients' lives, people receive disjointed care. Many times, teams in traditional health care settings tend to lessen personal responsibility and quality of care. Quentin Rae-Grant explains:

> A team may engage in a covert conspiracy to carry on subtle forms of … circular buck passing, especially passing the emotional buck non-stop around a circuit with no end; and the omnipresence of consensual validation may only serve to oblige no group member to think a problem through to resolution. Rather, some individuals may find in the anonymity of team membership, tacit permission to behave in less responsible ways than if the only appraisal available to them were self-appraisal.[23]

---

[23] Quentin Rae-Grant, "The Hazards of Team Work," *American Journal of Orthopsychiatry*, 38 no. 1 (January 1968): 5.

But, when caregivers work together as a team to communicate information vital to a patient's quality of life, the result is coordinated care that better meets the needs of the patient and family.

Hospice Care Uses Volunteers to Enhance Quality of Life

Hospice programs rely on trained, compassionate volunteers to provide extra sets of hands and ears, both for patients and families. To encourage the continued use of volunteers, Medicare requires hospice programs to provide documentation proving that volunteers contribute at least the equivalent of 5 percent of paid staff's hands-on patient care time.[24] With their varied interests and special talents, volunteers can greatly expand both the number and scope of services hospice programs can offer. Volunteers work in many capacities, including: helping in offices and with fundraising, providing transportation for patients, cooking

---

[24] Department of Health and Human Services, Centers for Medicare and Medicaid Services, "Appendix M, Guidance to Surveyors – Hospice," in State Operations Provider Certification, CMS.gov, accessed May 18, 2014, http://www.cms.gov/Regulations-and-Guidance/ Guidance/Manuals/downloads/som107ap_m_hospice. pdf.

or assisting with yard work, and staying in patients' homes for several hours at a time so caregivers can take breaks.

Hospice Care Provides Services Twenty-four Hours a Day

Hospice recognizes that dying patients and their families need care and support through nights and during weekends. Anyone who has experienced a serious illness or injury, surgery, or stay in the hospital knows that pain and discomfort seem to increase once the sun goes down. Symptoms like pain or itching can become intolerable.

Hospice care acknowledges the need for extra care and support by making on-call services available throughout nights and weekends. Staff members are on call at all times, with backup staff available if on-call staff is already responding to other calls. Hospice teams give the on-call numbers to patients and family members, encouraging them to call whenever problems or concerns arise. Sometimes, just knowing a nurse is on call is enough to comfort a family's fears. When family members do call, hospice staff can often handle the problems over the phone, but some situations require personal visits, whether five minutes or five hours.

The Basis of Hospice Care is Need

Hospice offers quality care to all terminally ill people, regardless of age, gender, nationality, race, creed, disability, diagnosis, availability of a primary caregiver, ability to pay, or place of residence. In almost every other component of the health care delivery system, patients must meet an increasing number of requirements to receive care. They must be very wealthy, very poor, or very well insured. They must be residents of particular communities for a certain length of time; they must suffer from particular diseases, and on and on.

But in hospice, the main criterion is terminal illness. Kathy L. Cerminara emphasizes that patients may wait too long before opting for hospice care. She contends,

> Patients ... having to renounce all curative efforts before Medicare will pay for hospice care may result in patient delay in accessing hospice care even if healthcare professionals have discussed that option in a timely fashion. Elisabeth Kübler-Ross identified five stages of dying, with the final one being acceptance; yet some patients never reach acceptance at all. To

renounce curative treatment would require accepting impending death, so requiring patients to reach acceptance before accessing hospice care, at best, postpones their initial election of Medicare payment for such services.[25]

Although the reimbursement and financial side of running hospice programs may seem unimportant to chaplains, this type of care is full of ethical dilemmas and difficult decisions that staff members and administrators around them must make on a daily basis.

Hospice Provides Bereavement Care

Hospice care provides bereavement services to help normalize the grieving process by giving supportive care and educating those in mourning about the cycle of grief. In most other components of the health care system, a patient's death signals the end of all interaction with the family. However, providing ongoing support for family members for at least a year following a patient's passing is a

---

[25] Kathy L. Cerminara, "Hospice and Health Care Reform: Improving Care at the End of Life," *Widener Law Review* 17, no. 2 (September 2011): 450.

basic concept of hospice care.[26] Chaplains prove critical in this vital process.

Bereavement services include: bereavement or grief support groups; memorial services; visits from chaplains, bereavement coordinators, and/or bereavement volunteers; community education programs on grief and bereavement; referrals for other services, including treatment of complicated grief; and periodic notes to let families know chaplains are praying for them.[27]

Hospice Provides Continuity of Care

Most hospice patients receive care in their homes. Medicare requires that hospice delivers 80% of the annual number of aggregate patient days in their residences.[28] However, home care is not always possible. Some patients require more intensive treatment for symptom control than caregivers can provide at home. In other cases, for

---

[26] Tammi Vacha-Haase, "The 'We Care' Program for Long-Term Care: Providing Family Members with Support Following the Death of a Loved One," *Omega: Journal of Death & Dying* 67, no. 1/2 (February 2013): 222.

[27] William J. Worden, "Bereavement," *Seminars in Oncology* 12, no. 4 (December 1985): 472-475.

[28] DHHS, CMS, "Appendix M, accessed May 18, 2014, http://www.cms.gov/Regulations-and-Guidance/Guidance/Manuals/downloads/som107ap_m_hospice.pdf.

family reasons, home care is not an option. When home care is not feasible, hospice programs face the challenge of ensuring that loving care follows their patients wherever they receive treatment.

Continuity of care is every hospice program's challenge and responsibility. Chaplains helping to meet the challenges of documentation, education, communication, and appropriate behavior can help every hospice program meet the challenge and responsibility of continuity of care.

Documentation: Comprehensive care plans including complete documentation of problems and prescribed treatments must accompany our patients to each health care setting to ensure continuity of care.

Education: Frequent in-service training must be provided for facility staff on topics such as pain and symptom control, hospice concepts of care, grief and bereavement, safety, the dying process, and other hospice related topics to help ensure continuity of quality care.

Communication: Open and continued communication with facility staff throughout a patient's stay must occur to help ensure continuity of care.

Appropriate Behavior: When chaplains interact with facility staff, we must model the types of behavior we expect them to use with our patients by showing compassion for their concerns and respect for their skills.

These responsibilities of each hospice team member also include that the hospice atmosphere of love and care surrounds our patients regardless of the setting in which they receive care.

Hospice Emphasizes Quality Patient Care, Education, and Research

In her work with the terminally ill, Saunders emphasizes the need for continued research and education to improve the quality of patient care.[29] Her commitment to maintaining detailed records of the efficacy of various pain and symptom control techniques allowed her to determine which treatments actually work and which do not. The results of her research led to tremendous improvements in the quality of life for her patients.[30]

Continuing quality assessment and improvement programs are also vital to enhancing care for the terminally ill. Joan Teno discusses the importance of quality of life concerning terminal patients suffering from dementia when she states, "The current research provides evidence of better family member perceptions of quality of care and qual-

---

[29] Stoddard, 123.
[30] Ibid., 241.

ity of the dying experience."[31] Saunders emphasizes asking, and more importantly, answering these difficult questions:

> Hospice is a place of meeting. Physical and spiritual, doing and accepting, giving and receiving, all have to be brought together … the dying need the community, its help and fellowship … the community needs the dying to make it think of eternal issues and to make it listen … we are debtors to those who can make us learn such things as to be gentle and to approach others with true attention and respect.[32]

Next, this chapter examines program models and legislation that caused the philosophy and concept of palliative care to grow in Western culture.

---

[31] Joan M. Teno, Pedro L. Gozalo, Ian C. Lee, Sylvia Kuo, Carol Spence, Stephen R. Connor and David J. Casarett, "Does Hospice Improve Quality of Care for Persons Dying from Dementia?" *Journal of the American Geriatrics Society* 59, no. 8 (August 2011): 1535.

[32] Stoddard, 14.

Hospice Program Models and Ownership

Hospice care in the United States is set up to follow a variety of different models established in response to the different needs of each local community. The predominant models are independent community-based programs, hospital-based programs, home health-based agency programs, and nursing home-based programs.

Independent Community-Based Hospice Programs: Independent Community-Based Hospice Care—This is the most common model used in the United States. In this approach, the organization provided home services to members of the community and contracts with a hospital or skilled-care facility for needed inpatient or respite care.

Independent Community-Based Free-Standing Inpatient Unit with Home Care—In this model, an organization operates a free-standing inpatient unit and also provides home care. Because inpatient hospice units are expensive to operate, this approach is not as common.

Hospital-Based Hospice Programs: Hospital-based hospice programs may be structured in one of several approaches. The hospital may operate a specifically designed hospice unit or offer hospice service to patients scattered throughout the facility. In some cases, hospitals offer hospice services in a free-standing hospice inpatient unit, which is usually located adjacent to the main hospital building or complex. In each of these hospital models, home care is an integral part of the hospice program's services.

Home Health Agency-Based Hospice Programs: In this model, a home health care agency offers hospice care services to its terminally ill patients and contracts with a hospital or skilled-care facility for needed inpatient or respite care.

Nursing Facility Based Hospice Programs: This model provides hospice care to terminally ill patients who live in a nursing facility. Care is delivered according to a Plan of Care developed by a hospice interdisciplinary team. The facility may need to contract with a hospital or skilled-care facility for needed inpatient care. Most nursing facilities contract with a hospice program to provide hospice care for their patients.

Regardless of the model, hospice programs must provide or arrange for inpatient care in facilities that meet Medicare standards. Either non-profit groups or for-profit groups of investors can own hospice program models. Both types of programs can deliver excellent or substandard hospice care. Quality of hospice care depends on many factors, including program goals, level of commitment to excellence in care, and quality of management, staff, and administrators. Over the years, it has become clear that both non-profit and for-profit Medicare-certified hospice programs can be financially sound, but quality of care is truly what makes the difference in meeting patient and family needs.

Rising global healthcare costs have led to recent changes in the United States, bringing significant health care reform measures. Congress recently passed both the Patient Protection and Affordable Act (signed into law March 23, 2010) and the Health Care and Education Reconciliation Act of 2010 (signed into law March 30, 2010). Leaders see these two legislative reform measures as the most sweeping health care reform measures taken in the past two decades. Although it is too early to discuss the consequences of these acts for hospice care, their expected impact warrants future discussion.[33]

---

[33] Noe, 232.

THE HOSPICE
INTERDISCIPLINARY TEAM

Hospice interdisciplinary groups include physicians, nurses, home health aides, social workers, counselors, chaplains, therapists, and trained volunteers. The Medicare Hospice regulations use the term "interdisciplinary group" in the regulatory text, but people can substitute the term "interdisciplinary team."[34] The hospice interdisciplinary team (IDT) is a highly effective, professional, caring, interconnected group in which the skills and expertise of each member are essential.

The role of the IDT is so important that the NHPCO requires programs to identify and maintain an appropriately qualified interdisciplinary team of health care professionals and volunteers. According to NHPCO, the teams' overall goal is to provide treatment that enhances comfort

---

[34] "Interdisciplinary Team," National Hospice and Palliative Care Organization, accessed September 9, 2013, http://www.nhpco. org/interdisciplinary-team.

and improves the quality of patients' lives, which means providing effective interventions for pain control and symptom management, as well as spiritual and emotional comfort for patients and family members. The standards require qualified health professionals to serve as team coordinators, ensuring ongoing assessments of the patients' and families' needs and the implementation of integrated plans of care.[35] The NHPCO's Standards of Practice for Hospice Programs further illustrates the importance of these teams. This regulatory document requires highly-qualified, specially-trained teams of hospice professionals and volunteers work together to meet the physiological, psychological, social, spiritual, and economic needs of patients and families facing terminal illness and bereavement.[36]

Hospice Interdisciplinary Team Members and Their Responsibilities

According to Medicare regulations, hospice interdisciplinary teams consist of four core members, each of whom must be present when the IDT reviews patient care plans. The four core members are a physician, a registered nurse, a social worker, and a counselor. Many hospice programs

---

[35] NHPCO, *Standards of Practice for Hospice Programs (2010)*, 214
[36] Ibid.

prefer to use a spiritual counselor (chaplain) as the fourth core member of the teams. In addition, most hospice programs include representatives from other disciplines in team meetings, such as volunteer and bereavement coordinators. Other specialized team members are also important in achieving the goal of excellent patient care.

The NHPCO's Standards of Practice for Hospice Programs include descriptions of team members' responsibilities.[37] Most hospice IDTs include the patients' attending physicians, the hospice physicians, registered nurses, nursing aides, home health aides, and homemakers, social workers, spiritual counselors (chaplains), volunteer coordinators, and specialized team members. To meet specific patient needs, the teams may include allied therapists, fine arts therapists, such as art and music therapists, dietitians, and pharmacists.

Qualified IDT members with appropriate credentials provide hospice spiritual services to patients. These caregivers base their spiritual care on initial and ongoing assessments of the spiritual needs of the patients and families, including histories of their religious affiliations, the nature and scope of their spiritual concerns or needs, and

---

[37] NHPCO, *Standards of Practice for Hospice Programs (2010)*, *213-216.*

the patients' families' desire for spiritual services. In fact, "current research illustrated the importance of religion and spirituality in the relationship between healthcare and the dying patient."[38]

Scholars further assert that when hospice providers offer spiritual care services from a cohesive perspective, they have a positive effect on how patients live out presence ministry. Reducing barriers facing chaplains as they strive to be collaborative members of interdisciplinary teams in the hospice setting is paramount to quality palliative care.[39]

Interdisciplinary Team Functioning and Expectations

Whenever groups of people work together as teams, whether at work, at church, in professional service clubs, or within families, several components of team functioning affect the way the groups operate. Jane Isaacs Lowe and Marjatta Herranen list these functions and describe them for people's understanding: team role expectations, methods of decision making, leadership styles, team commu-

---

[38] Daleasha Hall, Mary A. Shirey, and David C. Waggoner, "Improving Access and Satisfaction with Spiritual Care in the Hospice Setting," *Omega: Journal of Death & Dying* 67, no. 1/2 (February 2013): 102.

[39] Ibid., 106.

nication, group norms—what groups think are good and bad, and goals and tasks.[40]

Each chaplain plays several different roles in their everyday lives: hospice worker, spouse, lover, parent, child, sibling, and friend. As they attempt to fulfill each role, they commonly experience three role difficulties: role conflict, role ambiguity, and role overload. William L. White identified problems created by these role difficulties.[41]

Role Conflict: The various roles we fulfill frequently conflict with one another. Our role as a parent may require driving our children to school at exactly the same time our role as a hospice worker requires us to arrive at work. Our role as a family member may require us to stay home and care for a sick family member while our work role requires us to be at hospice to take care of others.

We also experience role conflict when we are expected to fulfill more than one role at a time. Can we effectively fill our role as a nurse and also provide social work services, supervise

---

[40] Jane Isaacs Lowe and Marjatta Herranen, "Interdisciplinary Team," *Hospice Education Program for Nurses,* U.S. Department of Health and Human Services Publication No. HRA 81-27, 1981, 423-450.

[41] William L. White, "Managing Personal and Organizational Stress in the Care of the Dying," *Hospice Education Program for Nurses,* U.S. Department of Health and Human Services. DHHS Publication No. HRA 81-27, 1981, 291-338.

staff, and train volunteers? Can we effectively fill our role as a social worker and also fill the roles of fund raiser, volunteer training, community educator, and marketing director? Can we work effectively as the program director and also provide social work services and act as team coordinator?

Role Ambiguity: Role ambiguity arises when: (1) We are uncertain about what the hospice program expects me to do. (2) The expectations for our role are not clearly communicated. (3) We are uncertain about what priorities should be. (4) We are unsure about how to complete a task, and (5) we don't know to whom who we report.

Role ambiguity increases tremendously if we are inadequately trained or receive poor orientation for our work role. Ambiguity and stress also increase when we are required to "blur" into other roles for which we have had no education or training.

Role Overload: Role overload occurs when we are expected to complete an excessive and unrealistic amount of work in a given time frame. Unrealistic personal expectations also contribute to role overload. Whether at home or at work, chaplains quickly become overloaded if they are expected to take on more and more responsibility without additional training or support.

Chaplains also discover that internal factors (what they think their role is and how they should act) and external factors (what other people think their role is and how they should act) influences the way they act in each role. Since role difficulties and conflicting role expectations interfere with their effectiveness and increase their stress, chaplains need to recognize and resolve difficulties as effectively as they can.

Interdisciplinary Team Leadership

Wise leaders vary their leadership styles to meet the needs of different circumstances. Although many leadership styles exist, each one is sometimes appropriate and effective and at other times inappropriate and ineffective. The most important fact is flexibility. Ken Blanchard and Phil Hodges state,

> leadership really applies to your behavior during implementation, because now your job is to be responsive to your people and help them be responsible for living according to the vision, accomplishing the goals, and taking care of the customers (patients, families, and caregivers).[42]

---

[42] Ken Blanchard and Phil Hodges, *Lead Like Jesus: Lessons from the Greatest Leadership Role Model of All Time* (Nashville: Thomas Nelson, 2008), 104.

Open teams discuss leadership style and its impact on the teams' effectiveness in delivering patient care. There are three common styles.[43] Under authoritarian leadership, the most powerful person in the team makes all the decisions. Although others may have input, the leader does not include them in final decisions. The democratic style involves equal participation. This style allows the expression of positive and negative feelings, prolonging the decision-making process, because everyone gets to express their opinions. Finally, a select few make group decisions under the oligarchic style. Group members may reverse or alter team decisions outside the official team meetings.

---

[43] U.S. Department of the Air Force, *Professional Development Guide*, AF Pamphlet 36-2241 (Washington, DC: Government Printing Office, 2011), 234.

SUMMARY

With a better understanding of the world of hospice and palliative care, people can take the next step toward allowing God's glory to shine brightly through them as hospice chaplains. The next section discusses the role of hospice spiritual care, keeping in mind the history of this movement and how it functions. It helps for chaplains to embrace the philosophies and concepts of care on which leaders establish this important form of health care and understand the operational models and team approach by which its success stands or falls. As part of interdisciplinary teams, hospice chaplains need to be catalysts for success, helping everyone in their quests to manage what can be a devastating part of life for so many.[44] However, with "Christ in you, the hope of Glory" (Col. 1:27),[45] chaplains can witness an amazing, incarnational impact as God's

---

[44] Lowe and Herranen, "Interdisciplinary Team," 423-450.
[45] All Scripture quotations, unless otherwise noted, are from the New International Version.

transforming power flows through them in the "ministry of presence" as they serve patients, families, and other caring professionals.[46]

---

[46] James E. Miller, *The Art of Being a Healing Presence: A Guide for Those in Caring Relationships* (Fort Wayne, IN: Willowgreen Publishing, 2001), 16-17.

HOSPICE SPIRITUAL CARE

Introduction

The call to work with the dying is a call to work with patients in a sacred place—the place of their death. It is a place where masks fall away as people stand on the doorstep of the unknown, letting go of everything familiar and learning to trust what is to come. As patients learn to let go, so do chaplains. They must let go of previously held notions about death and allow new insights and awareness to grow in the midst of their ignorance. They also must let go of the need to always be the teachers, becoming the students.

This section provides basic information about hospice spiritual care to chaplains by examining the psychosocial and spiritual aspects of pain; spiritual assessments and spiritual care plans; the roles of the spiritual care staff through their ministry of presence, grief, bereavement, and mourning; and staff grief and stress management, or caring for the caregivers.

Psychosocial and Spiritual Aspects of Pain

While working with the dying at St. Joseph's Hospice, Saunders remarked,

> Since our work at St. Joseph's is completely person centered, the criterion of success is not how our treatment is working, but how the patient is, what he is doing ... what he is being in the face of physical deterioration.[47]

Hospice care responds to the whole person: body, mind, and spirit. Saunders describes terminal pain as a combination of four interrelated types of pain—physical pain, emotional pain, social pain, and spiritual pain. She stresses the importance of first controlling physical pain since it affects people's abilities to cope with all other aspects of pain in their lives. In fact,

> ... excellent symptom control must surely be the first importance. Unless it is present nothing else is possible. One cannot adequately help a man to come to accept his

---

[47] Saunders, *The Moment of Truth*, 49.

impending death if he remains in severe pain, one cannot give spiritual care to a woman who is persistently vomiting, or help a wife and children say good-bye to a father who is so drugged that he cannot respond.[48]

Unrelenting physical pain increases social, emotional, and spiritual pain. Spiritual agony increases physical pain, making it more difficult to manage and control. Devastating emotional pain exacerbates pain in all other areas. This section examines some of the most common psychosocial and spiritual problems experienced by terminally ill patients and their families. Chaplains need to remember that this section separates the four types of pain only for purposes of discussion; in reality, they are inextricably bound. Each terminally ill patient is a whole person struggling to cope with the crisis of approaching death. The struggle exists on all levels of being: physical, emotional, spiritual, and social.

---

[48] Cicely M. Saunders, Dorothy H. Summers and Neville E. Teller, eds. *Hospice: The Living Idea* (London: Edward Arnold, Ltd., 1981), 92.

Spiritual Care

As he lay dying, Seneca of ancient Rome asked,

> Who is there in all the world who listens
> to us? Here I am, this is me in my naked-
> ness, with my wounds, my secret grief, my
> despair, my betrayal, my pain which I can't
> express, my terror, my abandonment. Oh,
> listen to me for a day, an hour, a moment,
> lest I expire in my terrible wilderness, my
> lonely silence. Oh God, is there no one to
> listen?[49]

In his last hours, Seneca asked for nothing more than the presence of another human being to listen to his fears as he faced death.

Spirituality is an essential dimension of being human that often lies dormant within people, even in those who are devoutly religious. For many, the spiritual aspect of their lives remains undeveloped until traumatic events,

---

[49] Saunders quotes Seneca to remind people that all who are dying experience a similar need. A short time of what she calls "true attention" can make death more bearable. Dame Cicely Saunders, "Spiritual Pain," *Journal of Palliative Care* 4, no. 3 (September 1988): 29-32.

such as terminal illness or deaths of loved ones, confront them with their own human fragility and impermanence.

Spiritual care is the treatment that focuses on relieving spiritual pain and suffering brought about by a sense of meaninglessness, the loss of faith, despair, failure, abandonment, betrayal, and injustice. Ministers base spiritual care upon careful assessments and specific interventions designed to alleviate spiritual pain, but unfortunately, as Hall states, "Spiritual care is often cut or under-funded when money is tight in organizations."[50] This limits the effect of "presence" ministry. When people learn to be "present," they need to understand that the strong desire to act, or to be effective, can also hinder their healing presence. As Miller argues, "The more we practice being completely present, the more natural it becomes."[51]

Ministry of presence provides spiritual care by listening to patients without trying to explain away their spiritual pain or package it in tidy bundles of religious dogma to make them more comfortable. Saunders reminds chaplains that members of the hospice team are "not there to take away or explain, or even to understand, but simply to 'watch' with our patients."[52]

---

[50] Hall, 106.
[51] Miller, 16-17.
[52] Saunders, "Spiritual Pain," 30.

Spiritual care is not something other-worldly that only selected members of the teams can provide. It involves sensitive listening, as well as the ability to remain present with patients as their spiritual struggles continue. Saunders also notes that all staff can provide the "gift of listening."[53]

As chaplains allow God's glory to shine through them while lending a listening ear, they provide answers many times as the struggle with the crisis of death occurs. They have unique opportunities to minister to dying patients, their families, caregivers, and other staff as well.

Spirituality versus Religion

Many people think spirituality and religion are identical. While there are similarities between the two, there are also important differences, which hospice chaplains need to understand before they can provide quality hospice care and allow God's glory to brightly shine through them. Some very religious people who observe all the rituals of their faith are not particularly spiritual, while some very spiritual people are not overtly religious and may not even be members of organized religion. In order to provide quality spiritual care in hospice, chaplains must under-

---

[53] Ibid., 31.

stand the differences and similarities between religion and spirituality.

Religion/Religious

Scholars usually describe religion as an institutionalized pattern of beliefs, dogmas, sacred writings, traditions, rituals, practices, and ethical beliefs that exist within the context of a structured religious community. Some of the world's major religions include Hinduism, Buddhism, Judaism, Christianity, and Islam. Within each of these major religions are various subgroups, sects, or denominations.[54]

The word "religion" comes from the Latin word *religio* or *re-ligere*, which means to re-link, to re-connect, or to rebind to the cosmos.[55] At their deepest cores, religion and spirituality have similar goals—to reconnect believers with themselves, with others, with God, and with the cosmos. Saunders reminds people that religious beliefs/practices can provide support at the deepest level for many hospice patients, but for others, religion may be a source of disquiet

---

[54] A more complete explanation of various religious beliefs and divisions or sects within them can be found in Warren Matthews, *World Religions*, 7th ed. (Belmont, CA: Wadsworth, 2013).

[55] Robert K. Greenleaf, *Servant Leadership: A Journey into the Life of Legitimate Power and Greatness*, 25th anniversary ed. (Mahwah, NJ: Paulist Press, 2002), 231.

or guilt. She suggests spirituality is much broader and more inclusive than religion.[56] Although the basic goals of various religions are similar, religion sometimes divides people instead of bringing them together. In order to provide the "gift of listening," palliative care chaplains must remain sensitive to the religious and spiritual needs of patients and their families.

Major World Religions and Their Views
of Death and Immortality

Many people go through their lives giving little thought to death until they are faced with either their own death or the death of a loved one. Then, suddenly, all the questions previously ignored or shoved into the background begin to surface. What happens after death? Does our existence end? What is the purpose of death? How are we supposed to prepare to die?

Answers to such questions bring meaning, not only to our deaths but also to our lives. Kenneth Kramer suggests all cultures have developed rituals and beliefs to provide answers to the seeming absurdity of death.[57] From the

---

[56] Saunders, "Spiritual Pain," 30.

[57] Kenneth Paul Kramer, *The Sacred Art of Dying: How World Religions Understand Death.* (Mahwah NJ: Paulist Press, 1988), 178.

beginning of time, cultures and their religions have developed traditions surrounding the dying process, disposal of corpses, and funeral rites. In addition to ritual practices, each religious tradition also developed sacred stories to help believers understand the significance of death.

Kramer tells us religions view death as a sacred act, a final ritual, and a last opportunity to discover life's ultimate meaning and purpose. Religious traditions ritualize the dying process to mind their adherents of the "impermanence of life, and that whatever lies on the other side of death is real, if not infinitely more so, than life itself."[58]

Death related rituals, myths, and sacred stories help answer questions about death and provide us with a sense of victory over death's finality. Kramer also asserts that each of the world's religious traditions teaches how to die successfully by showing us to view dying as a process that involves both dying and being reborn. During the sacred act of dying, death is viewed as dying to what we have been and being reborn to what we will become. In this sense, dying becomes one of the greatest and most sacred acts and arts of life, and one of the most difficult to cultivate.[59]

---

[58] Ibid., 1.
[59] Ibid.

Our views about death affect our journey through the dying process. For this reason, hospice chaplains need basic understanding of major world religions and their basic attitudes, beliefs, and rites surrounding death and dying. However, as we review the death-related beliefs of five major world religions, we need to remember that many striking variations of belief exist within each one. While most Christians, whether they are Roman Catholic or Protestant, share a basic underlying attitude about death different from that of Buddhists or Hindus, remarkable differences in belief and practice exist among these Christian groups. Beliefs and rituals surrounding death and dying even differ within various Protestant denominations. For this reason, the best technique for helping patients die meaningfully is communicating with them about death-related beliefs and practices.

The Three Views of Death as a New Beginning

Most world religions view death as both an ending and a beginning—an ending of life as we know it and the beginning of one of three broad types of a new existence.

> *Heaven/Hell* – The concepts of Heaven and Hell are characteristic of three major world religions: Judaism, Christianity, and Islam. After death, one

continues to exist and are either rewarded by God with eternal existence in Heaven (a place of paradise) or are punished with eternal existence in Hell. However, differences in interpretation exist, particularly among Jews, many who believe that one lives on in community memory rather than actually continuing to live an individual existence after death.

Rebirth – Although Hindu and Buddhist religious traditions differ in many ways, the concept of rebirth is characteristic of them both. After death, these religions believe that one is reborn (reincarnated), but not necessarily as our individual selves. Belief in rebirth is even becoming popular in the United States among some liberal professing Christians even though this is contrary to what the Bible teaches.

Spirit – The concept of returning to an essential spirit is characteristic of indigenous religions, including those of Native Americans. In most of these religions, which can include New Age religious beliefs, one returns to an essential or cosmic spirit after death. This belief is also becoming more common among some Christians who do not hold the Bible as absolute.

In addition to these three very basic descriptions of belief, an extraordinary number of individual beliefs about death exist. The British historian Arnold Toynbee explained that belief in the re-embodiment of the dead is an essential component of the belief systems of all Zoroastrians, Jews, Christians, Muslims, Hindus, and Buddhists. The first four teach that a human being lives only a single life, but that the soul survives after death, disembodied, and at some unpredictable future date, becomes re-embodied in order to undergo the Last Judgment, and according to God's judgment, will enjoy either physical bliss in heaven or physical anguish in Hell. Hindu and Buddhist teachings assert a soul is reborn many times until it reaches a state of oneness and perfection, at which time, the process of being reborn through the cycle of *samsara* ceases.[60]

Death and the Afterlife – Different Religious Views

The following descriptions of various religious traditions and the views of death and the afterlife come from several noted experts on World Religions. Due to space

---

[60] Kramer, 178.

limitations, the descriptions provide only a very general overview.

Hinduism - Hinduism is the religion of over nine hundred thirty-five million people, most who live in India. It is an amalgam of traditions, rituals, devotionals, and philosophical systems built up over the past four thousand five hundred years. Polytheism is the basis for much popular Hindu worship. Brahma, the Hindu creator of the universe, serves as the first god of the Hindu trinity, the other two being, Vishnu, the preserver who is associated with grace, and Shiva, the dissolver or destroyer.[61]

The basis of Hinduism is the unity of ultimate reality. One's view of the world, which comes through our senses, seems to consist of a multitude of differences, apprehensions, and anxieties, but all this is an illusion (*maya*). In order to become aware of and participate in the one true reality, which is called Brahma, we must rid ourselves of our illusions and ignorance (*avidya*). By achieving the realization that our individual selves are only a manifestation of the one true self, which is called Atman, we attain enlightenment (*moksha*). The knowing of the true self is not a mere intellectual knowing, but is enlightenment of one's

---

[61] Warren Matthews, *World Religions*, 7th ed. (Belmont, CA: Wadsworth, 2013), 71-72.

entire being. If we fail to recognize the one true self, we remain tied to the wheel of birth and rebirth (*samsara*) and return to this world in another reincarnation. The attainment of enlightenment is possible through spiritual practices such as yoga.[62]

Hindu Spiritual Disciplines - Four common spiritual disciplines (paths) or yogas[63] are:

1) Jnana Yoga: The way of knowledge employs philosophy and the mind to comprehend the unreal nature of the universe. Through meditational practices, one can achieve a deathless identity in life and comprehend the unreal nature of the universe.

2) Bhakti Yoga: The path of devotion, love, and emotional self-surrender. The goal of bhakti yoga is single-hearted devotion to a god and offering everything to this god. The bhakti welcomes everything that happens as a gift from the gods.

3) Karma Yoga: The way of action or works, which performs all things without regard for personal gain or personal attachment to the results of those

---

[62] Huston Smith, *The World Religions*. (New York: Harper Collins, 2009), 26-50.

[63] Matthews, 81-88.

actions. Those who perform the proper rituals every day and at the turning pints in their passage of life can fulfill all their religious obligations and lead to the goal of release. The Vedic sacrifices are at the heart of the path of works.

4) Raja Yoga: The way of physical discipline trains the physical body so the soul can be free. A person who is serious about approaching their god must concentrate on cleanliness and strong control over bodily desires.

Hindu view of death and the afterlife - The final goal of Hinduism is to escape the endless wheel of birth, death, and rebirth (*samsara*) by realizing Atman the deathless Self. When the body dies, Hindus believe the Self continues to live; in fact, the secret of death is the realization of the supreme Self, which is hidden in the heart. Realization of the one true Self is attained not by preaching or sacrifice but through meditation and grace. Those who die unaware of the one true, eternal Self are reborn in another evolutionary state as determined by their actions according to the Law of Karma. Those who die aware of the eternal, true Self are at last released from the cycle of birth, death, and rebirth (*samara*). The Self (*Atman*) is joined to Brahman in the cosmos and eternal peace is theirs.

In Hinduism, death is natural and unavoidable, but even death itself is not real, only union with Brahman and identity with the eternal true Self is real. The focus of Hindu sacred writings is on this eternal Self, how to recognize it, and how to realize it. Hindus realize this eternal, true Self through the spiritual practice of yogas, which helps them join the Atman in each of them to the Brahman in the cosmos. Most Hindus believe they have many incarnations (lives) ahead of them before attaining Moksha (union with Brahman). However, some sects believe a gracious divinity, such as Vishnu, can help them along their path of existences more quickly.

Hindus preparation for death and the afterlife - As death approaches, a Hindu is surrounded by religious rites and ceremonies to provide support through the death process. A son or relative puts water from the Ganges River in the dying person's mouth to bring peace and comfort. Family and friends sing devotional prayers and chant mantras to reassure the dying person with comforting words and the gentle tone of the chanting. After death occurs, the body is washed, anointed, and dressed in new clothes, and the hair and beard are trimmed. Hindus believe cremation is the most spiritually beneficial way of disposing of a corpse because it allows the soul to quickly begin its journey. The body is put on a funeral pyre and three fires are lit. After cremation, any remaining bones are buried or cast into a river.[64]

Buddhism - Buddhism is the religious and philosophical system of some five hundred million people, most of whom live in Asia. Buddhism is based on the life and teachings of Siddhartha Gautama, who may have lived in the sixth century BC. Becoming the Buddha ("enlightened one" or "one who woke up") he rejected certain features of his native Hindu culture, particularly the caste system, animal sacrifice, and strict asceticism.[65]

Buddhist spiritual disciplines - The Buddha essentially presented a middle path between the two extremes of self-indulgence and self-mortification. These four noble truths[66] of his enlightenment are:

1) Life is suffering (*dukkha*) or dissatisfaction
2) The origin of suffering lies in craving, grasping, and desiring (*tanha*), and the cycle of rebirths is perpetuated by the desire for existence.
3) The end of suffering is possible through the cessation of craving.

---

[64] Kramer, 38-39.
[65] Matthews, 109-110.
[66] Ibid., 117-118

4) The way to cease desire and attain escape from con-
tinual rebirth (*samsara*) is by following Buddhist
practices known as the Noble Eightfold Path (see
below).

The Buddha developed his primary teachings the same
way a doctor diagnoses an illness. What are the symptoms?
What causes the suffering? Can anything be done to alleviate the patient's distress? What is the treatment that can
bring relief or cure? He further taught that our selfish desires
are rooted in our dualistic delusions about the self. When
one abandons desire, then they can pass from the world of
individual existence into Nirvana, which is incomprehen-
sive liberation from suffering and the absence of self. This
is a state of total cessation.

According to Buddhist teachings contained in their
three baskets of sacred writings (*Tripitaka*), Buddha was
a Hindu prince who renounced a life of luxury to seek
spiritual enlightenment after witnessing four sights which
caused him great unrest. After studying various spiritual
practices for several years, he meditated for many days and
nights, literally staving himself and enduring many painful
body positions, during which time he experiences temp-
tations of body, mind, and spirit, but eventually "woke
up" with the answer. Buddha then spent over forty years

teaching the wisdom of the Four Noble Truths as well as the Noble Eightfold Path, which includes: 1) Right View, 2) Right Aim, 3) Right Speech, 4) Right Action, 5) Right Living, 6) Right Effort, 7) Right Mindfulness, and 8) Right Concentration.[67]

Buddha stressed constantly that religious life does not depend upon doctrines or formations. He encouraged his followers to surrender their dependence on external teachings, including his own, and devote themselves to achieving unconditional, selfless compassion. As he lay dying from dysentery from eating spoiled pork in 483 BCE, he encouraged his followers to concentrate on working out their own salvation and reminded them that each person is responsible for their own enlightenment. Buddha rejected the notion that he was a philosopher, guru, or someone to be worshipped, and when asked about his role, would only say, "I am awake."[68]

Buddhist view of death and the afterlife - According to Buddhist teachings, death is the result of breaking apart of the temporarily bonded material of which we are composed (*skandhas*). In Buddhism, there is no eternal Self, or Atman, to achieve as there is in Hinduism. In Buddhism,

---

[67] Ibid.
[68] Smith, 82.

there is simply awakening. While Hindus reject the idea of the immortality of the body, but retain the idea of immortality of the soul (*purusha*), Buddhism rejects both concepts. Buddha taught that no soul exists to migrate from one life form to another. When a person dies, matter, sensations, perceptions, mental formations, and consciousness (*skandas*-five strands) dissolve, but the life stream continues even though no underlying self or permanent entity remains or exists.

Some Buddhists compare the process of dying and being reborn to a candle flame being transferred from one candle to another. When the flame of one lit candle is touched to the wick of an unlighted candle, the light passes from one candle to another, but the actual flame of the first candle does not pass over. Buddhism teaches that "rebirth is a process of the transformation of the entire evolutionary process with all its possibilities and probabilities."[69]

Escape from rebirth is possible by achieving Nirvana. Nirvana is not a place, an idea, or a state of being unconscious or asleep. Nirvana is what is left when illusion, ignorance, desire, and attachment have fallen away. Buddha taught that Nirvana is incomprehensible and can only be known mystically, by direct perception. Nirvana is libera-

---

[69] Kramer, 51.

tion from suffering, the extinction of desire, the elimination of ignorance, the absence of self, and the end of all desire to enter the cessation of all things.

Buddha rarely addressed the question about life after death. Instead he suggested that asking about life after death is asking the wrong question; one should ask how we can be liberated from human suffering. Buddhism views ignorance rather than sin as the roadblock which keeps people from Nirvana, which is a transcendent and permanent state.

Buddhist preparation for death and the afterlife - The death practices among Buddhists vary widely from country to country, but Buddha's teachings emphasize that a person's state of mind while dying is of great importance. For this reason, the dying person is surrounded by family, relatives, friends, and monks who recite sacred texts and repeat mantras to help the dying person achieve a peaceful state of mind. After death, the body is washed and dressed in burial clothes and cremated. Some Buddhists believe the dead person's conscious soul remains in or around the body for several days, so monks are invited to chant scriptures to assist the dead person's passage to the spiritual world and to relieve the mourners' fears.

Tibetan Buddhists are a deeply religious people who developed the *Tibetan Book of the Dead,* a well-known guidebook that contains very detailed instructions for dealing with the period between death and rebirth. The book is studied during life and then read to the dying person so liberation from rebirth can be achieved and the Pure Land attained.

Judaism - The three religions that form the bedrock of western culture are Judaism and its two offshoots, Christianity and Islam. For the first time in history, Jewish theology coupled a belief in one god with emphasis on the importance of ethical righteousness.

Judaism is based on the belief in one universal god as the creator of the universe. Judaism interprets history as God's covenanted choice of the Children of Israel to be the vehicle of his revelation and ultimate rule. God's revelation was handed down from Mt. Sinai when the Ten Commandments were given to the deliverer, Moses. Over many centuries, the laws of Moses were codified and made applicable to most situations of life. Judaism expects a messianic age when God's rule will be manifest in the world. Modern Judaism has divided into five groups in modern times: orthodox, conservative, reformed, Hasidic, and Zionistic.[70]

---

[70] Matthews, 245-270.

Jewish view of death and the afterlife - According to Jewish teachings, our eternal experience in the hereafter is determined by our moral behavior and attitudes toward God, although even the evilest person is offered the possibility of repentance. The notion of an afterlife is not well-developed in the *Tanak* (Jewish Bible), so teachings about individual salvation and heavenly existence are not prominent in most Jewish belief systems.

However, the Jews, in particular Orthodox Jews, still hope for the coming of the Messiah, who will establish God's kingdom on earth and deliver eternal judgment to all. In Jewish beliefs, the hope for reward is largely communal rather than personal and stresses eternal existence for the entire Jewish race and the whole of creation, rather than eternal existence for an individual. Judaism teaches that one's moral life here on earth is considered our most proper concern, with final judgments being left to God.

Within the large body of Jewish Theology, a wide range of beliefs exist about the afterlife, from no specific view to a belief in the resurrection of the body and the immortality of the soul. In earliest Jewish writings, no clear description of an afterlife exists, however both life and death are explained as necessary and created by God. In these writings, death is viewed not as a punishment for sin, but as a part of creation. At death both the body and soul return to their source. As the writer of Ecclesiastes in the *Tanak* states, "There is a time for everything, and a season for every activity under the heavens" (Ecclesiastes 3:1). Therefore, each person has a time to live and a time to die.

Later Jewish writings describe humans as being born with a pure soul and a sacred body, which are interdependent and have no existence apart from one another. This belief contrasts with the Hindu view that our souls maintain an existence independent of our bodies. Later, Jewish writings also describe a time of great calamity on earth, after which the Messiah will establish a perfect society. Orthodox Jews believe in a personal Messiah, but many other Jews view the Messiah not as a person who is an individual savior, but as a time of collective redemption for the Jews. In some later writings, Jerusalem is described as being rebuilt after the Messiah's arrival, at which time the bodies of the dead will be resurrected and rejoined with their souls. Death will no longer exist as we presently know it, and the righteous will rise to be with God eternally. The wicked will not rise, and will be annihilated from memory.

In Jewish belief, one attains a place in heaven by living in accordance with God's laws. When one dies, their evil acts are weighed against the good and righteous acts committed in life. If righteousness outweighs evil the person is assured heavenly eternity. For that reason, most Jews concentrate their energy on right living and performing good acts rather than on developing an elaborate afterlife theology. The religious Jew need not fear death, because to them, it is sacred and a part of God's creation. All righteous will be raised again when the Messiah arrives in judgment.[71]

Jewish preparation for death and the afterlife - In Jewish culture, a dying person must be attended to constantly. Just before death occurs, the dying person makes a confession and prays for forgiveness. From the time of death to the funeral, the body is never left unattended. After death, a son or relative closes the corpse's eyes and mouth, and washes and dresses the body, which Orthodox Jews bury as quickly as possible because they do not practice embalming or cremation. At the end of the funeral service, relatives recite a mourner's prayer, the Kaddish.

For seven days after the funeral, family members observe a time of intense mourning, during which they pray and read from Jewish sacred texts. The Kaddish is recited every day, a practice that continues for the next twelve months.[72]

Christianity - Christianity developed from the Jewish belief in one God and the importance of ethical righteous-

---

71 Matthews, 283.
72 Kramer, 134-138.

ness. Christianity is the religion of over two and a quarter billion people who accept Jesus of Nazareth as the Christ, the incarnation of God, and worship him as the Son of God and savior of mankind. The virgin birth of Jesus and his life, teachings, death, and bodily resurrection are described in the four sacred books of the New Testament called the Gospels.

The exact date of Jesus' birth is unknown but many believe it was around 4-6 BC, but his crucifixion occurred during the early first century. Jesus was a Jewish religious teacher and prophet whose message was the coming of God's kingdom, the need to prepare for it, and an ethic of love, mercy, and justice. During his three-year ministry, Jesus performed many miracles and healed the sick, and even raised the dead. Then he was tried by the Roman Empire and crucified.[73]

Christians believe Jesus is a historic Jewish person who lived, died, and was bodily resurrected and then like the Jewish prophet Elijah, he ascended to heaven. As a Jewish prophet, teacher, and healer, Jesus, like Isaiah portrayed God as a loving Father, a view very different from both the jealous God of the most of the Jewish writings and the unpredictable and often spiteful gods and goddesses of

---

[73] Matthews, 289-298.

pagan Rome. In Christian theology, Jesus is viewed as the Messiah, the Christ (anointed one), and one of the three parts of the Trinitarian nature of God that is composed of the Father, the Son, and the Holy Spirit. Jesus is also described as the divine son of God whose bodily resurrection after death is the central tenant of the Christian faith.

For Christian believers, the resurrected body is fully, eternally human. This differs from the Hindu belief that after death, an enlightened soul enters into Brahman and from the Buddhist belief that physical bodies disintegrate after death, but the life force becomes one with Nirvana. The fundamental difference between Jesus and the Hindu gods, including Krishna, who is the incarnation of Vishnu, is that Hindus accept the mythological expression of their gods, while in Christianity, Jesus must be understood through the eyes of actual history.

In the second century, the early church safeguarded its beliefs again heresy by convening synods and ecumenical councils to formulate creeds, define the nature of the Trinity of God, establish the canons of the Bible, and establish the apostolic succession. In the eleventh century, disagreement over papal authority resulted in schism and led to the establishment of a separate Greek Orthodox Church and Roman Catholic Church. The Reformation of the sixteenth century led to the formation of many Protestant sects and another schism developed which resulted in the division of western Christianity into Protestantism and Roman Catholicism.[74]

Christian view of death and the afterlife - Christians' attitudes toward death and dying stem from their belief in the reality of Christ's bodily resurrection, which is seen as the center of history and the fulfillment of God's promise of everlasting life. Christian belief in eternal life is of primary importance and each of the many forms of Christianity developed elaborate and detailed views of life after death. Eternal life in heaven is described as flowing from two sources: the perfect knowledge and love of God and loving compassion for all persons in God's family. For Christians, the possibility of life in heaven and eternal existence are the result of moral behavior and attitudes, as well as the saving grace of Christ.

New Testament teachings, which are the basis of Christian theology, describe four key aspects of death: death is a consequence of sin; death is a temporary separation of the body and soul; death to sin is birth into eternal life; and the dead will be raised and judged at the second coming of Christ.

---

[74] Ibid., 301-316.

For Christians, death is the result of sin, which entered the world through one man and woman: Adam and Eve. Paul, an early Christian, described sin as the opposite of holiness and righteousness and as the turning away from the divine gift of love. At death, each Christian believes they will be judged and their soul will be sent to either heaven or hell. Catholic Christians also believe in purgatory. When Christ returns to earth, a second, final day of judgment will occur during which time the bodies of the dead will rise up again and rejoin their souls. Christ will then make his final judgments and eternal life will be rewarded to those who committed themselves to Jesus and served their neighbors, and the rest will be sent away to eternal punishment.

In some more liberal Christian theology, heaven and hell are not restricted to particular places where we go after death, but can also be viewed as states of mind which we experience in our present lives.[75]

Christian preparation for death and the afterlife - Many different funeral practices exist among various Christian groups, and some are more elaborate than others. The early church developed the sacrament of "last rites," which is usually accompanied by two other sacraments: confession and communion. Each sacrament offers liturgi-

---

[75] Kramer, 145-151.

cal Christian believers both an opportunity for experiencing the real presence of Christ and ritualized participation in the death and resurrection of Christ. These practices continue today in the Catholic, Orthodox, and liturgical Protestant traditions. Such sacraments are meant to provide these Christians with the courage to die, knowing Christ will support and transform them. During the sacrament of the sick, a priest prays for the dying and anoints them with holy oil. As death approaches, prayers are offered that embody the source of the believer's faith.[76]

Evangelical Christians also have differing approaches for preparing for death that include offering prayers, hymns, and sharing stories of faith that strengthen friends and families during their time of grief.

Islam - Islam is one of the world's fastest growing religions and is now the belief of more than 1.5 billion people. Its religious and social system is based on the teachings of the prophet Mohammed. The Koran, the holy book of Islam, records the will of Allah as it was revealed to his chosen prophet Mohammed by the angel Gabriel. The Koran also outlines strict codes of behavior and punishments for their non-observance.

---

[76] Ibid., 151-155.

Mohammad's earliest preaching stressed four points: the sole sovereignty of Allah, the sinfulness of idolatry, the certainty of resurrection with rewards of heaven and the punishments of hell, and his own divine vocation as the final prophet for Allah.

Mohammed lived from 570-632 AD, and differed with the religious beliefs of his countrymen, including: the believers in traditional Arab religions for what he thought was their idolatrous worship; the Jews for what he believed was their re-interpretation of the universal religion of Abraham into an exclusive nationalistic system; and the Christians for what he believed were their pagan beliefs in a virgin birth and a triune God. Mohammed believed that the concept of the Trinity, which the Christian Church adopted in 451 AD, was a rejection of the belief in the oneness of God.

The first stated belief (*Shahada*) of all Muslims is, "There is no other God but Allah and Mohammed is his messenger." Muslims recognize and worship Allah as the creator of all life, and must honor, not worship, Mohammed, who revealed Allah's divine word in the Koran. The Koran's account of the creation, temptation, and fall of Adam are similar to those found in Jewish and Christian sacred texts.

There are two major divisions in Islam. These came about as a result of differing views of who should have followed Mohammed as the religious and civil leader of the Muslims. These groups, the Sunnis and the Shi'ites, have different practices and views of succession of leadership from the prophet. Shi'ites, who comprise a minority of Islam (ten to fifteen percent), regard themselves as the most pious, holy, and God-inspired members of Muhammad's family. They are waiting for Muhammad's grandson, Husayn to return in the last judgment as Mahdi to set the record straight. Sunnis, who are the majority of Muslims, do not believe the Shi'ite claims. They acknowledge Abu Bakr who was elected after Muhammad's death as their first caliph.[77]

Muslim view of death and the afterlife - For Muslims, creation, death, and resurrection are sacred and linked. Life involves preparing the soul to be worthy to pass through the state of death and progress to life after death. In Islam, death is a transition from this world to eternity.

Muslims view heaven as a place of delight and hell as a place of torment. On the final day of reckoning, Allah will judge each person according to his/her acts. Salvation in Islam depends on a person's words, deeds, and attitudes, however, repentance is possible and can turn an evil person toward virtue. Muslims recognize different individu-

---

[77] Matthews, 335-357.

als have been given different abilities and various degrees of insight into the truth of Allah. Each person is judged according to their individual situation and every person who lives according to the truth will achieve a place in heaven. However, those who are acquainted with the truth of Islam and reject it will be shown no mercy.

The Koran describes a barrier that separates the living from the dead; the deceased have no way to return to earth and no way to be reincarnated. As with Judaism and Christianity, the dead wait for the day of resurrection and judgment, at which time they will rise from their graves in the midst of cataclysmic events. After rising from their graves, each will be judged according to the number of good and bad entries that have been recorded by secretary angels in a set of heavenly books. Unbelievers will be cast into hell.[78]

Muslim preparation for death and the afterlife - Islamic practices surrounding death vary from country to country, but generally, the dying person is positioned on his back with his head facing Mecca. The room is perfumed, and anyone who is unclean or menstruating leaves. Islamic scriptures are read by the dying person, or a relative, and the dying person repents of all earthly sin. After death,

---

[78] Kramer, 157-163.

the corpse's mouth and eyes are closed, the feet are tied together, and the body is covered with a sheet.

Reciting from the Koran near a dead body is unlawful, but other prayers are offered. The body is cleaned, perfumed, wrapped in white cotton, and carried in a plain wooden coffin to the burial ground, where it is removed from the coffin and buried immediately. All those present cover the body with flowers and dirt and recite prayers. As with Judaism, embalming is not allowed. Mourners say their prayers for the dead while standing because bowing and prostration are not allowed except in worshipping before Allah.[79]

Spiritual/Spirituality

Religion is a part of spirituality, but spirituality is much broader than any one particular religion. Although difficult to define, like the most important concepts in people's lives, the spiritual dimension is what inspires individuals and gives meaning to their lives. In many languages, the word for spirit is also the word for life, breath, or wind.

Spirit is usually thought of as: "(1) the essence, unifying force, or vital principle of each person, (2) the power and process of going beyond our present life's situation, or

---

[79] Ibid., 164-166.

(3) the power and process of relating to and connecting with one's self, others, nature, the cosmos, and God."[80]

The definition of the word *spiritual* is as follows: "Pertaining to the innate capacity to, and tendency to seek to transcend one's current locus of centricity, which transcendence involves knowledge and love."[81] The definition terms include innate capacity, tendency, seeking, current locus of centricity, transcend, greater knowledge, and greater capacity to love.

Innate capacity: all humans have a spiritual component that is developed in different degrees at different times in a person's life.

Tendency: each person has an internal motivation toward spirituality, but the motivation can vary from total repression of anything spiritual during some periods of our lives to an over-riding concern with spirituality during other times of our lives.

---

[80] *Collins English Dictionary-Complete & Unabridged,* 10th ed., sv. "spirit," accessed April 16, 2014, http://dictionary.reference.com/browse/spirit.

[81] Chandler, et al. developed a working definition of "spiritual." At first, their definition sounds somewhat awkward, however taking time to think about this approach can help scholars define the word "spiritual" with much more clarity. See Cynthia K. Chandler, Janice Miner Holden, and Cheryl A. Kolander, "Counseling for Spiritual Wellness: Theory and Practice," *Journal of Counseling and Development* 71 (November/December 1992): 168-175.

DR. DOUGLAS G. SULLIVAN

Seeking: we are unable to make spiritual experiences happen, but we can create an environment that increases our openness to spiritual experiences and allows us to incorporate those experiences into our lives.

Current locus of centricity: refers to our frame of reference, or how we view life events. For instance, when we view all life events in terms of how those events affect our personal wants and goals, we operate from an egocentric from of reference. Going beyond our current frame of reference means we are able to expand our frame of reference as we grow spiritually.

Transcend: "moving beyond" to a higher or broader frame of reference.

Greater knowledge: a higher or broader world view that is more inclusive and focuses on unity and what we have in common, rather on differences. Increased knowledge results in a greater sense of purpose and meaning in life that is less dependent on personal accomplishment or material possessions and more dependent on growing awareness.

Greater capacity to love: a benevolent acceptance of what "is" combined with greater motivation to bring about good. It also means great acceptance of other people as they are and responding to others more authentically.

Spiritual Development

Spiritual development is an ongoing process in which people open up to the spiritual aspects of their lives. Bruce Demarest asserts that increased development starts during spiritual beginnings and involves feeling securely orientated, which heightens people's sense of inner strength. Next, spiritual trials painfully dislocate people. This increases their sense of unfolding mystery. Finally, they formulate their sense of harmonious connection as they experience spiritual renewal, securely relocating in the place where true relationship results.[82]

Isabelle M. Dearmond emphasizes that "working at the hospice is an experience of spiritual growth, especially when the participants were already aware of their spiritual life."[83] From these stages of growth, inner strength, unfolding mystery, and harmonious connection have great impact on people's lives as chaplains help them connect spiritually. A closer examination of these concepts reveals the characteristics behind inner strength, unfolding mystery, and harmonious connection.

---

[82] Bruce Demarest, *Seasons of the Soul: Stages of Spiritual Development* (Downers Grove, IL: InterVarsity Press, 2009), 14-15.

[83] Isabelle M. Dearmond, "The Psychological Experience of Hospice Workers during Encounters with Death," *Omega: Journal of Death & Dying* 66, no. 4 (December 2012): 292.

Inner strength: increasing our inner resources for coping with spiritual crises and experience a sense of transcendence. Transcendence brings a greater sense of peace and unity with all of life.

Unfolding mystery: becoming more aware that the meaning and purpose of our lives goes beyond everyday events. As we face life's uncertainties, tragedies, losses, joys, successes, and failures, one is able to cope better with life's ambiguities and uncertainty. We have a sense of the unfolding mystery of our lives. Our sense of hope, patience, acceptance, and peace maintains us, even when there are no easy answers.

Harmonious connection: a sense of belonging to and connecting with ourselves, others, the cosmos, and God in life-giving ways. We feel harmoniously connected with the oneness of the cosmos, God, or a higher power.

In her excellent textbook on palliative care nursing, Madalon O'Rawe-Amenta notes a tendency of hospice team members to feel agitated or irritated when people mention the subject of spirituality, particularly when they suggest nondenominational or nontheistic approaches to spiritual assessment and intervention.[84] Neil Holm carries

---

[84] For a more detailed discussion of these concepts, see Madalon O'Rawe-Amenta and Nancy L. Bohnet, *Nursing Care of the Terminally Ill* (Boston: Little Brown and Company, 1986).

this concept even further, discussing the role of chaplains and the importance of spiritual development. He contends,

> This is why spiritual development, spiritual growth is so important. Spiritual growth is not a matter of making chaplains more right with God, not a matter of becoming more holy people for their own satisfaction, convenience, comfort, well-being, and happiness. Spiritual growth matters because as chaplains serve their spirit engages with the spirit of the other person; their identity partly resides in each person with whom they enter into relation.[85]

Milton W. Hay warns chaplains to be aware of their own spiritual traps. He further suggests that broadening their spiritual views may be their most significant task in hospice care if they are going to truly build bridges to connect with people and allow a healing presence to flow.[86]

---

[85] Neil Holm, "Practising the Ministry of Presence in Chaplaincy," *Journal of Christian Education* 52, no. 3 (December 2009): 34.

[86] Milton W. Hay, "Principles in Building Spiritual Assessment Tools," *The American Journal of Hospice and Palliative Care* 6, no.

Dealing with all types of pain is important. But all too often, traditional healthcare settings address only physical pain. Sylvia Lack and Robert Buckingham demonstrate that viewpoint with the following assertion:

> Among health care professionals and those concerned with the issues of death and dying, there is far too much talk about psychological and emotional problems of the dying patients, and far too little about the physical comfort of these patients. Any group concerned with service to the dying should be talking about smoothing sheets, rubbing bottoms, relieving constipation, and sitting up at night. Counseling a person who is lying in a wet bed is ludicrous. If people are cared for with common sense and basic professional skills, with detailed attention to self-evident problems and physical needs, patients and families can themselves cope with many of their emotional crises. Without pain, well-nursed, with bowels controlled, mouth clean, and

---

5 (September/October 1989): 25-31.

a caring friend available, the patient will be able to bring the psychological problems into manageable perspective.[87]

For many years, a majority of dying patients had no one to help them sort out what really matters. And now, with so many hospices, there is still a trend to neglect spiritual, psychosocial, or emotional pain and only deal with physical symptoms. Levine charges:

> In many hospices, the predominant goal is the alleviation of distress, the palliative care of the patient. There is little encouragement to cut through identification with the body as being who we really are or the mind as being the whole reality. Hospices can have a tendency to overlook dying as a means of spiritual awaking.[88]

Hospices can address this problem by focusing on all aspects of pain and providing comfort in the way that

---

[87] Sylvia A. Lack and Robert W. Buckingham, III, *First American Hospice: Three Years of Home Care* (New Haven: Hospice, Inc., 1978), 91.

[88] Levine, 169.

Saunders originally intended. This is why the healing ministry of presence is so important, making accurate spiritual assessments and developing spiritual care plans to meet patients' and families' true needs critical in alleviating spiritual pain.

Spiritual Assessments and Spiritual Care Plans

Developing a spiritual plan of care brings some great challenges. Chaplains must accurately assess the presence and degree of each patient's spiritual pain and then develop care plans that respect the patients' levels of spiritual development, spiritual concerns, religious beliefs and rituals, values, and cultural observances.

Spiritual Care Plans

A spiritual care plan is an individualized assessment of spiritual problems detailing specific interventions to relieve those dilemmas. Like physical and psychosocial care plans, chaplains must base the spiritual care plan on effective evaluations and realistic short-term goals.

Since spiritual pain affects every aspect of people's lives, spiritual care staffs need to share information about patients' spiritual suffering with other interdisciplinary team members. Only by sharing information can the team adequately provide comprehensive care. When discussing patients' spiritual problems during hospice team meetings, or when writing notes in patients' charts, spiritual counselors can provide needed information while still respecting their request for confidentiality. Such clinical notes respect the patients' desire for privileged communication but alert other interdisciplinary team members about the high levels of spiritual pain possibly affecting other areas of care. The goal of the spiritual plan of care is to relieve spiritual pain, which in turn reduces physical, emotional, and social pain and restores patients' sense of peace, connection, dignity, and worth. Relieving spiritual pain frees patients to reconnect with family, friends, the cosmos, and God.

Spiritual Assessments

The spiritual assessment is the cornerstone of effective spiritual care plans. Spiritual assessments help chaplains determine the spiritual needs of both patients and their family members. As spiritual counselors interact with patients and families during the assessment process and throughout the delivery of spiritual care, chaplains need to remember three critical aids to effective interaction: autonomy, language, and presence.

Autonomy: Chaplains must remain sensitive to the spiritual and religious values, meanings, and beliefs of each patient/family and refrain from imposing our own religious beliefs and spiritual practices on any patient or their family.

Language: A powerful tool. The words chaplains use can bring us together and help us explore spiritual issues, but they can also separate us. Using religious language that offends a patient's religious beliefs interferes with spiritual assessment and the delivery of spiritual care. A lack of sensitivity to a patient's religious or spiritual framework results in division. Patients assume we are unable to hear their pain without judgment because chaplains can be insensitive to the language of their religion, especially if it is different than our own. As we interact with patients and their family members, we must use language that respects their religious beliefs and practices.

If we constantly refer to Jesus or the New Testament while assessing a Jewish patient's spiritual pain, our language reflects our insensitivity to this patient's beliefs and interferes with exploring spiritual issues. If we continuously refer to the need for a personal relationship with Jesus or the importance of being "saved" while assessing the spiritual pain of a patient who belongs to a liberal religious group, our language once again reflects insensitivity and poses a barrier to exploring important spiritual issues.

When making spiritual assessments, sensitivity to a patient's spiritual and religious beliefs is vital. When making physical assessments, we enhance communication by using our patient's terms for various body parts. We ask patients which medicines or treatments they used in the past to relieve physical pain. In the same way, we can enhance communication during the spiritual assessment process by reflecting our patient's religious language and inquiring about which spiritual or religious practices and beliefs that they found helpful or meaningful in the past. In this way, effective spiritual counselors signal our sensitivity and willingness to listen and learn.

Presence: Interactions with patients and family members should reflect the importance of listening, silence, compassion, attention, and discussion.

Five Principles of Hospice Spiritual Assessment

Hay describes five principles that should guide the development of spiritual assessments.[89] First, spiritual assessments should encompass both religious and nonreligious belief systems. Spiritual assessment language also needs to address more than religious affiliation or the presence of psychological problems. Spiritual pain may not be separately identifiable from psychosocial pain until it reaches a certain level of discomfort. Chaplains must also

---

[89] Hay, 25-31.

recognize that each patient has the capability to heal spiritually. Spiritual and religious practices can enhance their ability to heal. Finally, the spiritual assessment process should recognize that spirituality occurs in the context of patients' religious or spiritual communities and that enhanced spirituality increases their inner resources for dealing with the challenges of life, including dying. Spirituality's objective is to give meaning to people's lives.

Hay also recommends that spiritual assessments should address each of the four challenges listed below: (1) the patient/caregiver's spiritual suffering, (2) the patient/caregiver's inner resources for dealing with spiritual crisis, (3) the patient/caregiver's belief system, and (4) the patient/caregiver's religious needs.[90] Every member of the hospice interdisciplinary team needs to have a basic understanding of each of these four areas.

Role of the Spiritual Care Staff: Ministry of Presence

Saunders describes the pain of meaninglessness and the importance of being present with patients as they struggle to find true meaning in their lives. This "ministry of pres-

---

[90] Ibid.

ence" is paramount if chaplains truly reflect God's glory to impact patients' or families' experiences. Saunders explains:

> A feeling of meaninglessness can be the hardest pain of all for a dying person to bear. Now, you can never impose your own meaning upon another person and his situation, but in a place like hospice where other people are convinced of the meaning of living and dying, it is easier to find your own way. Sometimes another patient is more help than anyone else. Sometimes the staff has to bear their inability to understand, to feel as if they are not helping at all, yet still go on staying close to the patient. We tend to feel that if we are bringing nothing, then we had better stay away.

> But I think that is just the moment when we have simply got to stay. And if this is the moment when the patient feels that there is no meaning in life and that the weariness of it all is more than he can cope with and we are feeling hopeless too, well,

we are very much on the same level there. In that place where you share helplessness—there, perhaps, you can help more than you realize.[91]

Hospice chaplains help patients discover meaning in their lives by listening and encouraging them to talk about their accomplishments, the goals they met, the high points in their lives, their contributions, the ways in which they helped others, and the joys and sorrows of their lives. Life review accomplished by spiritual counselors who allow God's glory to flow through them is tremendously important when establishing a sense of meaning and a feeling that one's existence has made a difference in this world.

The Chaplain's Role in Palliative Care—
Ministry of Presence

In their excellent book about the work of chaplains, Naomi Paget and Janet McCormack link the chaplain's ministry of presence to the manifest presence of God:

The presence of God in the person and ministry of the chaplain empowers the cli-

---

[91] Saunders, "The Moment of Truth," 74.

ent to healing and wholeness … [I]n part-
nership with the presence of God, chaplains bring calm to chaos, victory over
despair, comfort in loss, and sufficiency in
need. Chaplains practice the presence of
God through prayer, rites, rituals, listening, the spoken word, the holy scriptures,
and acts of service.[92]

An important part of ensuring quality of life for dying
patients is assisting them with the search for meaning in
their lives and in their deaths. As they accompany their
patients in their search for meaning, chaplains can encourage those with religious beliefs to find strength and hope
within the context of their own religious traditions. For
patients with no religious affiliation or those for whom
organized religion is a source of disquiet rather than peace,
chaplains can assist them with the search for meaning by
helping them explore basic spiritual issues within a context
of peace and love as they endeavor to serve them through a
ministry of presence.

---

[92] Naomi K. Paget and Janet R. McCormack, *The Work of the
Chaplain* (Valley Forge, PA: Judson Press, 2006), 28.

According to Miller, "Healing presence is the condition of being consciously and compassionately in the present moment with another or with others, believing in and affirming their potential for wholeness, wherever they are in life."[93] This "healing presence" that spiritual counselors offer patients, families, and caregivers impacts lives and allows the glorious presence of Christ to flow through them as they build appropriate relationships with those in crisis.

Hospice chaplains have priceless opportunities to minister not only to dying patients, but to their families, caregivers, and other staff as well. Miller further explains,

> The more you are a healing presence in the midst of everyday events, the more you come to appreciate that the common ground on which you stand with another is pulsing with all that is divine. You realize that holiness is at work as you consciously and compassionately accompany others … as people experience healing presence, they change … such changes are not yours to own or to keep for yourself— they are meant to ripple out in all direc-

---

[93] Miller, 12.

tions, touching family, friends, colleagues, patients, clients, anyone with whom you come into contact ... this transformation takes place right before your eyes, through commonplace happenings, in everyday relationships, in all sorts of families, in every kind of organization, and with every type of human endeavor.[94]

Holm also discusses the importance of presence ministry for chaplains by stating,

... the chaplain and the public may perceive that nothing is happening, but for the experienced spiritual care provider, the art of 'hanging out' with patients, clients, victims or team members becomes an intentional event that leads to providing a calm presence during times of stress or chaos ... presence may seem insignificant, but presence is the grace gift that chaplains bring to the human encounter.[95]

---

[94] Miller, 69-72.

[95] Neil Holm, "Toward a Theology of the Ministry of Presence in Chaplaincy," *Journal of Christian Education* 52, no. 1 (May 2009): 9.

Chaplains can only share this "grace gift" if they have first experienced for themselves. To truly make a difference and to allow God's presence to flow through them, chaplains also must be healthy, balanced, and full of God's Holy Spirit so this precious resource can minister through them and change the lives of their patients, their families, and other caregivers.

The Chaplain's Role in Palliative Care— Ministry of Presence to the Team

An old Latin aphorism says: *Nemo dat, quod non hat,* or "You cannot give what you do not have." This saying is particularly true when providing spiritual care. In order to help those who are suffering spiritually, chaplains need to develop a firm sense of their own spirituality. As hospice team members work with the dying, constantly surrounded by their pain, they frequently experience the challenge of their own spiritual beliefs, a fact which is normal and expected. On occasion, particular patients or family situations will throw chaplains completely off balance.

Chaplains must remain sensitive to the spiritual pain experiences of other team members. Saunders uses the term "wounded healers," reminding chaplains of the need to support the entire team to do hospice work.[96] She also reminds caregivers that Carl Jung, one of the first psychoanalysts to recognize the power of the spiritual aspect of people's lives, referred to "the urge to set to rights whatever is still wrong,"[97] which chaplains often see in those who are dying.

Just as chaplains who provide spiritual counseling to help their patients "to set to rights whatever is still wrong,"[98] they need to be very sure they are taking time to help themselves. Taking care of the caregivers is a primary role of the spiritual caregivers. Providing the ministry of presence is paramount in supporting each other in palliative care.

---

[96] Saunders, "Spiritual Pain," 31.

[97] See Carl G. Jung, "The Soul and Death," in *The Meaning of Death*, ed. H. Feifel (New York: McGraw-Hill, 1959), 3-15.

[98] Ibid., 11.

GRIEF, BEREAVEMENT, AND MOURNING

People often use the terms "grief," "bereavement," and "mourning" interchangeably, but in reality, these words actually have quite distinct and different meanings. William Worden and James Monahan do an excellent job differentiating these concepts.[99] Therese Rando also defines some of these words most commonly used when discussing grief.[100]

Mourning refers to cultural reactions to loss and includes customs, rituals, and prescribed time periods for grieving. Various customs of mourning imply there is no one right way to grieve. People express grief reactions according to their personalities and the cultures in which they live. Glenn Davidson says, "The idea of mourning is

---

[99] See William J. Worden and James R. Monahan, "Caring for Bereaved Parents," in *Hospice Care for Children,* 3rd ed., ed. Ann Armstrong-Daily and Sarah Zarboc Goltzer (New York: Oxford University Press, 2008), 181-200.

[100] Therese A. Rando, "Concepts of Death, Dying, Grief and Loss," *Hospice Education Program for Nurses*, U.S. Department of Health and Human Services. DHHS Publication No. HRA 81-27, 1981, 129-130.

extremely old and has been preserved in two of humanity's most ancient languages. The root meaning in Sanskrit is 'to remember,' and in Greek is 'to care.'"[101] When death occurs, families mourn their loss. They are bereaved and involved in the process of grieving. Some cultures observe special times of mourning.

The Process of Grief

When terminally ill people are dying, families and friends begin to journey through the process of grief which involves letting go of the person who died and learning to adjust to a new reality that no longer includes that cherished person. When they expect death, friends and family members begin preparing for their loss during an initial phase called "anticipatory grief."[102] As family members think about how their loved one's death will affect their lives, they anticipate the loss and begin to grieve. After the death occurs, family members continue the process of adjusting to a new environment which no longer contains the person they loved.

---

[101] Glenn W. Davidson, *Understanding Mourning: A Guide for Those Who Grieve* (Minneapolis, MN: Augsburg Publishing House, 1984), 6.

[102] Robert Fulton and Julie Fulton, "A Psychosocial Aspect of Terminal Care: Anticipatory Grief," *Omega* 2 (1971): 91-99.

Hospice chaplains need to become familiar with the symptoms of both complicated and uncomplicated grief. Their ability to provide quality hospice care depends on their capacity to make effective assessments and appropriate interventions in spiritual and emotional care. The important thing to remember is that grief is not a contest. Each patient and family walks the journey of grief in their own way. While most people are able to accept their loss in styles unique to their own personalities, and at their own pace, there may be times when hospice chaplains need to attune themselves to provide extra help in the bereavement process.

Although every relationship is unique and mourners grieve in their own ways, some reactions are common in the grief process. Elisabeth Kübler-Ross[103] identifies coping mechanisms used by those who are grieving as they try to adjust to loved ones' deaths. As chaplains work with those who are grieving, they need to remember mourners may or may not experience the reactions Kübler-Ross suggests. When people experience such responses, they do not occur in any special order, and they may also happen simultaneously.

The concept of grief occurring in stages is full of difficulties. Sometimes chaplains think their responsibilities

---

[103] See Kübler-Ross, *On Death and Dying.*

include pushing grieving family members from one stage to another. They become concerned when grievers are angry for "too long" or their depression lasts for weeks. Many times, the best intervention for grieving individuals is the ministry of presence—supportive listening and reassurance as they experience their feelings of grief. Miller asserts that effective hospice chaplain must remain completely present, "staying awake to each unfolding moment. You give yourself fully to the present instant, letting go of what was, and choosing not to anticipate what will be. You don't *do* presence—you *are* presence."[104]

As with the stages or reactions to dying, chaplains need to remember the stages, reactions, or coping mechanisms of grief can co-exist, come and go, and rapidly replace one another. Concerns about the stage concept of grief led to the development of other ways to describe the grief process. Some experts use three broad categories when discussing the grief process: avoidance, confrontation, and re-establishment.[105]

---

[104] Miller, 15.

[105] For a much more detailed explanation of these concepts, see Therese A. Rando, "Concepts of Death, Dying, Grief and Loss," *Hospice Education Program for Nurses*, U.S. Department of Health and Human Services. DHHS Publication No. HRA 81-27, 1981, 113-230.

The normal symptoms of grief do not feel normal at all to most people. In fact, some of the most commonly experienced symptoms can be frightening. In her article, Rando refers to common indicators of grief identified by E. Lindemann,[106] C. M. Parkes,[107] and others. Hospice chaplains need to normalize the symptoms of grief by providing mourners with education and reassurance that the presence of such symptoms does not mean the grievers are crazy.

---

[106] See Erich Lindemann, "Symptomatology and Management of Acute Grief," *American Journal of Psychiatry* 10 (1944): 141-148.

[107] See Colin M. Parkes, "Effects of Bereavement on Physical and Mental Health: A Study of the Medical Records of Widows," *British Medical Journal* 2 (1964): 274-279.

Determinants of Grief

One of the goals of palliative care is the identification of potential high-risk grievers, so all hospice staff, and especially hospice chaplains, need to know something about the determinants of grief and their influence on family members' reactions to the deaths of loved ones. Worden identifies five determinants of grief that affect people's reactions to a death:[108] (1) nature of the attachment, (2) mode of death, (3) historical antecedents, (4) personality variables, and (5) social factors.

Nature of the attachment. The most intense and difficult grief reactions often occur when the attachment between the bereaved and the deceased was very strong; when the deceased was needed to support the survivor's sense of self-worth and esteem; when the survivor was highly dependent on the deceased; or when the relationship was highly ambivalent.

Mode of death. The manner of death influences the grief response. A sudden death is often more difficult to grieve than one with advance warning. The natural death of an older person is usually not as difficult to grieve as the accidental death of a young child, a murder, or a suicide. However, we must remember that relationships are unique.

---

[108] Worden, "Bereavement," 472-475.

The bond between a child and grandparent may be stronger than the child's bond with a parent, especially if the grandparent raised the child.

Historical antecedents. How the griever handled previous losses and how well those losses were resolved can also help predict the griever's response to the current loss. A history of major depression or other emotional disorders may contribute to a more difficult period of mourning. Multiple losses can also increase the probably of a difficult grief process. If a family member has experienced several recent losses, the accumulation of grief can make the process of resolution more difficult.

Personality variables. A person's ability to tolerate emotional pain and anxiety, and the ability to express feelings can influence reactions to death. Mourners with a history of adequate coping with other stresses, including other deaths, are more likely to be able to cope with the current death. However, if previous losses included deaths of elderly friends or grandparents, the ability to cope with those deaths may not predict the ability to cope with the unexpected, violent death of a child. Other personality variables affecting reactions to a death include introversion and extroversion. Extroverts want to express their grief to others. They find comfort in company and support groups. Introverts, on the other hand, tend to experience grief in a more solitary manner. They find solace in being alone or with a close friend. They may not talk about their grief for a while.

Some grievers experience their grief on a feeling level while others express their grief on a more cognitive or thinking level. Grievers with "feeling" personalities cry and want to be in touch with the emotions of grief. Those with more cognitive personalities tend to process grief in a more logical, orderly manner. "Thinkers" may not want to dwell on something that cannot be changed, such as the death of a loved one. Each of these ways of grieving, and many others are appropriate ways to share grief. As hospice chaplains, we must allow mourners to experience grief in ways that fit their personality.

Social Factors. The availability of support from family, friends, and the work place can also influence our reactions to death. Coping with a death may be more difficult if the mourner has moved frequently, is estranged or geographically separated from other family members, or is not involved with a church or other supportive network.

Lack of cultural guidelines and rituals for grieving also affect our reactions to death. Cultures with established rituals and models for mourning, especially rituals that mark the time of mourning as a special phase, provide guidelines about what is normal during the grieving process.

Understanding these determinants can lead to early identification of family members at risk, so bereavement services can be targeted to these family members who are most likely to experience difficulties with the grief process.

Four Tasks of Grief

Although there is no right way to go through the process of grief, William Worden also identifies four tasks grievers must accomplish to successfully negotiate the grief process.[109]

The four tasks are as follows: (1) accepting the reality of the loss, (2) experiencing the pain of loss, (3) adjusting to an environment without the deceased, and (4) emotionally relocating the deceased and moving on with life. Like reactions to grief, there is no set order in which people must accomplish the tasks. However, to begin the process, grievers must accept the reality of their losses. This is the first task.

Task One: Accepting the Reality of the Loss. Accepting the reality of the loss means working through the tendency to deny the death occurred and accepting, both intellectually and emotionally, the fact that the death occurred.

---

[109] William J. Worden, *Grief Counseling and Grief Therapy,* 4th ed. (New York: Springer Publishing Company, 2009), 39.

This means acknowledging that the dead person will not be returning to this life.

Task Two: Experiencing the Pain of Loss. Experiencing the pain of loss means giving up attempts to minimize grief and to acknowledge the painful emotional reactions that accompany all loss, especially death. Since none of us likes to experience painful feelings, we are tempted to cut short the pain of grief. We want to get it over with and then get on with life. Without actually meaning to, friends, other family members, and institutions also try to cut the process short. Places of employment want workers back and fully functional in just three days. Caught in their own feelings of helplessness, mourners need to experience the painful feelings of grief.

Task Three: Adjusting to an Environment Without the Deceased. Adjusting to a new environment that no longer includes the deceased is a painful process that takes time to accomplish. At first, a mourner may not realize all the roles filled by a loved one. If the deceased was a spouse, the mourner may have lost a friend, lover, bill-payer, bed-warmer, car washer, cook, or grocery shopper.

In addition to adjusting to the external environment, those who are grieving must also adjust to changes in their internal environment. Mourners are accustomed to relating to the deceased in many ways, including emotionally and mentally. For example, when we notice a favorite store is having a sale or we hear a joke, we often think, "I can't wait to tell (name of deceased)!" If the person we want to tell is the person who died, we experience waves of grief as we realize once again that the person we are used to talking and sharing with is no longer physically present. Adjusting our thought patterns is a part of adjusting to life without the person we love.

In the midst of the confusion and pain of the grief, mourners may experience a great deal of resentment about having to learn tasks that used to be their partner's job. Learning how to work the washing machine, write checks, iron, manage a business, or arrange social occasions can seem overwhelming. However, moving from a state of helplessness to a state of responsibility for learning new skills is required to complete this task. With time, mourners often experience feelings of pride about their growing independence and new skills.

Task Four: Emotionally Relocating the Deceased and Moving on with Life. Emotionally relocating the deceased and moving on with life means the mourner begins to redirect his/her emotional energy from the person who is dead to those who are living, to satisfying hobbies, and/or to other activities. Successful relocation means taking up or lives again.

During the grieving process, mourners may think the decision to become reconciled to grief means forgetting the person who has died, so they struggle to keep their loved one in the present by putting their own lives on hold. However, becoming reconciled to a loved one's death does not mean forgetting. Reconciliation means adjusting our relationship with the dead person from one of presence to one of memory. We begin to incorporate a painful new reality into our lives and make a decision to say yes to life.

As a hospice chaplain, one can support the relocation process by reassuring grieving family members that a decreasing intensity of grief is normal. We may also need to remind them that feelings of sadness can resurface during anniversaries, birthdays, and holidays, or when other deaths or life crises are experienced. At such time, our grief freshens; once again we feel sad, our throats tighten, and tears fall. However, as we heal we are able to experience our feelings and then let them go more easily. Instead of stabbing us in the heart, our grief becomes a dull ache.

Eleven months after the death, as the first death date anniversary approaches, grievers frequently experience intensified grief. The grieving person may or may not be aware of the approaching date, but begins to relive all the painful events of the previous year on either a conscious or unconscious basis. Working through renewed grief is another aspect of grief work and presents an additional obstacle grievers must negotiate as they continue on their journey through grief.

As the first year of mourning draws to a close, some grievers experience another hurdle. Because a year has passed, many grievers begin to think they should be over it and wonder why they still hurt. They begin to feel bad about feeling this way and wonder if they are grief backsliders. They may be reluctant to begin a conversation about the deceased because too much time has gone by. Survivors may feel uncomfortable or even embarrassed about wanting to talk about the deceased and their continued grief.

The eleventh month hurdle presents an opportunity of intervention with a phone call or visit from the hospice chaplain. Grievers may particularly welcome contact with their hospice chaplain and an opportunity to talk about their loved one, the pain they still experience, and the progress they have made in their journey of grief.

Expressing Grief is Important

Until recently, many thought that controlling feelings and hiding grief was the right way to grieve. If people lost control of themselves, they should do it in the privacy of their own homes. Currently, there is no scientific proof that people who deny their grief will get cancer or go crazy. Some mourners grieve openly and in public while others grieve quietly and in private. Some grievers may be in such denial they are unable to face their losses at all.

Hospice chaplains have a tremendous responsibility to correctly assess patient and family needs, provide a supportive presence, educate, and make referrals when appropriate. Unless the choices patients and families make adversely affect their health and well-being in serious ways, the chaplain's job is to accept their choices without judgment and to walk with them in this journey of grief so God's presence can bring healing to their lives.

Complicated Grief

Alan D. Wolfelt suggests using the term "complicated," rather than "pathological" or "abnormal," when describing a particularly difficult grief process. He notes the term "complicated grief" is more helpful and life-enhancing, because it suggests grievers have the "knowledge and tools to uncomplicate the mourning process."[110] James R. Monahan says complicated grief is a "grief process"

---

[110] Alan D. Wolfelt, "Toward an Understanding of Complicated Grief: A Comprehensive Overview," *The American Journal of Hospice and Palliative Care* (March/April 1991): 28-30.

interfered with or complicated by beliefs of the grieving individuals or behaviors of others. Those complicating factors interfere with the grief process.[111]

Experts on grief, including Worden and Davidson, have also identified the following behaviors as warning signs of complicated grief:[112] persistent thoughts of suicide, chronic grief or long-term depression, abuse of alcohol or other drugs, delayed grief, exaggerated grief, absent or masked grief, and failure to provide for basic survival needs.

Persistent thoughts of suicide. After the death of a loved one, those who are mourning may wonder if they want to go on living. Periodic thoughts of suicide are normal. However, persistent thoughts of suicide or forming a plan to commit suicide, require immediate referral to a spiritual counselor or hospice chaplain. This attention and treatment can save lives.

Chronic grief or long-term depression. Today we know the process of grief takes longer than we thought. Although some mourners are able to complete the tasks of grief and

---

[111] See Worden and Monahan, "Caring for Bereaved Parents," 181-200.

[112] A more complete explanation can be found by examining Glen W. Davidson, *Understanding Mourning: A Guide for Those Who Grieve* (Minneapolis, MN: Augsburg Publishing House, 1984) and William J. Worden, "Bereavement," *Seminars in Oncology* 12, no. 4 (December 1985): 472-475.

take up their usual activities after nine months to a year, some mourners need much more time. Depending on the circumstances of the death, intense grief may last for one to two years. The first death anniversary can produce an acute grief reaction that can last for weeks. A sudden or violent death, one that was completely unexpected, and multiple losses may require two or more years for completion of the tasks of mourning.

When grief remains static and the levels of depression, anger, or guilt remain unchanged for months, the mourner may have become stuck in the grief process and need extra help. In most instances, mourners realize something has gone wrong and seek help. If not, the hospice chaplain needs to intervene as appropriate.

Abuse of alcohol or other drugs. Substance or alcohol abuse is a common risk factor for complicated grief. Referral is the appropriate intervention.

Delayed grief. If grief is linked to an earlier loss that was insufficiently mourned, complicated grief is more likely.

Exaggerated grief. During intense periods of grief, most mourners experience some dysfunction and are temporarily unable to function at previous levels. However, when normal responses to grief become so exaggerated the griever is completely dysfunctional, additional help or referral is appropriate.

Absent or masked grief. Sometimes grief appears to be absent at the time of the loss, but later appears as a medical or psychiatric symptom. Referral is needed.

Failure to provide for basic survival needs. The inability of mourners to provide for their own basic survival needs, such as safety and nutrition, is a warning signal of complicated grief. Support and intervention are needed.

Hospice chaplains can assist patients and their families with the grief process in many ways. They must remember that almost anything they say that comes from the love of God in their hearts will be the right thing to say. They must allow God's manifest presence to flow from them and impact the lives of others as only He can.

As hospice chaplains, we can assist our patients and their families with the grief process in the following ways:

1) Help both the dying patient and family understand that grieving begins even before death occurs. The patient grieves over the coming loss of life, separation from all that is known, and the loss of control. Family members grieve the coming death of their loved one and all the changes that it implies. Education about the process of grief can help patients and families cope with the wide range of feelings they may experience. Education

will also help family members better accept the gradual separation that sometimes occurs during the terminal stages of life.

2) Encourage the family/patient to say their good-byes. Help them to say anything that needs to be said before the death actually occurs. Support patients and family members as they reminisce together, forgive each other for past hurts, review family albums, and express love and concern. Encourage life review. If appropriate, ask survivors about early memories they have of the deceased, including how they met. If fitting, inquire about the high and low points of their relationship and what will be missed or not missed.

3) Encourage family members to be with the patient both during the death and for a while afterwards. After the death, suggest family participation in a brief ritual, such as holding hands and saying a few words about the person who has just died. Support and facilitate their decision to pray, sing, or reminisce.

4) Support conversation about the deceased. Help family share memories by asking them to tell about times they shared together. Memories mixed with tears often lead to memories mixed with laughter. Express your own feelings and memories and,

remember, hospice staff and chaplains are allowed to cry. Say the name of the deceased; family members want their loved one's name to be remembered.

5) Become familiar with normal grief and remind the family a wide range of feelings is normal. Help them to understand that they are not going crazy.

6) Know the signs of complicated grief and make referrals as needed.

7) Remember that parents who have experienced the death of a child are among those who will have the most difficulty with the grief process.

8) Refer mourners to support groups, such as Compassionate Friends for parents of children who have died, or Survivors of Suicide for those who have experienced the suicide death of a loved one.

9) Encourage expressions of grief, such as talking and weeping.

10) When talking with family members, provide good role modeling by taking the initiative. If you feel helpless, admit you do not have all the answers. A statement like, "I'm not sure what to say or do, but I do want you to know that I'm here and I care about you," can do wonders.

11) Remember grief is a process that takes varying amounts of time; frequently two years or lon-

ger for some types of deaths. Do not put your own time limit on someone else's grief. Support mourners for as long as needed. Grief cannot be avoided or rushed.

12) Remember, some of us are upset by expressions of grief in others because of our own fears of death or the expression of emotion.

13) Be cautious when trying to explain or make sense of a death. Beware of saying, "It is God's will," or "it is all part of God's plan." We need to be very careful how one uses the word "God." Many have no idea what God may have wanted or not wanted. After a death occurs, children frequently make up an image of God as an avenger who took away their parent or grandparent.

14) Also be cautious about using religious language or scripture, themes from scripture, or church teach-ings. Many families and caregivers are not religious and do not have knowledge of what these things mean. Listen carefully to the family and take your cues from them. Ask which words and concepts they have found comforting in the past. Remember, when family members use religious words such as God, their concept of God may be quite different than yours as a chaplain. Respect and honor what

they find comforting, rather than assuming what comforts you will also comfort them.

15) Remember, grief may also be accompanied by guilt, anger, or hostility. If these reactions occur, remind the family they are normal. Getting angry at the person who died, God, themselves, and almost everyone else is usual. Keep in mind the family will probably respond to the death just as they have responded to other difficult situations. If family members have a pattern of expressing hostility toward one another in times of crisis, they will usually respond to a death the same way. Family behavior that has taken years or generations to form will not change overnight.

16) Recognize clichés and avoid them. Be careful saying, "time heals" because time by itself does not necessarily heal; it can also destroy, alienate, and separate. Grief is an emotional wound that needs cleaning, verbalization, and expression. Also beware of saying things like, "God never sends us more than we can stand." This families' observation could be that the world is full of people who have been crushed by the tragedies in their lives. Your job as a spiritual caregiver is to walk with

them and provide hope through God's transforming presence in the midst of their crisis.

17) Also remember that nonverbal communication is important. A pat or embrace, or simply sitting beside a person in silence can facilitate the healing process. Also understand that different people have a different tolerance for touching. Some are uncomfortable with any touch, others are warm and embracing. Take your cues from the family and remember as a palliative care chaplain to remain professional but approachable.

18) Help family members accept their feelings as valid and do not try to talk them out of what they are experiencing. If they feel guilty, accept their guilt without saying, "Oh, you should not feel that way!" Listen, accept what they say, and validate their feelings. When the time is right, as their chaplain, you can then help them sort out unrealistic expectations of themselves.

19) Try not to be upset by the intensity of emotions. After outbursts have ended, reassure mourners that intense emotions are normal and to be expected when someone close to us dies.

20) Remember, I emphasize again, that almost anything you say that comes from the love of God in

your heart is going to be the right thing to say. Do not struggle for the right words. Just be there and walk with them in this tender and sacred moment. Allow God's glorious presence to flow from you and impact their lives as only he can.

Scholars discuss the effectiveness of hospice care to deal with complicated grief:

> Hospice programs are specifically designed to provide end-of-life care in order to manage distressing symptoms, maximize patient quality of life, address needs of family, and is touted as the optimal care model for patients with advanced lung cancer. Family members report greater satisfaction with hospice care than care in other settings, and improved family well-being and functioning.[113]

---

[113] Betty J. Kramer, Melinda Kavanaugh, Amy Trentham-Dietz, Matthew Walsh, and James A. Yonker, "Complicated Grief Symptoms in Caregivers of Persons with Lung Cancer: The Role of Family Conflict, Intrapsychic Strains, and Hospice Utilization," *Omega: Journal of Death & Dying* 62, no. 3 (September 2010): 204.

We learn how to grieve from our family and our culture. Western society values strength as the best way to cope with grief. This response interferes with the griever's need to experience the pain of grief. Lack of knowledge can complicate the grief process as well as the deritualization of American culture. Our culture's rejection of the use of rituals such as funerals and an official period of mourning interferes with the grief process.

Hospice Bereavement Services

Bereavement counseling includes emotional, psychosocial, and spiritual support and services provided before and after the death of patients to assist with issues related to grief, loss, and adjustment. For many hospices, social workers or chaplains provide pre-death assessments for patients and families with bereavement staff providing support following death.[114]

Because the grieving process can be so difficult for many people, palliative care provides hospice bereavement support services from the time of admissions through the twelfth or thirteenth month after the death of hos-

---

[114] "Medicare Hospice Conditions of Participation Bereavement," National Hospice and Palliative Care Organization, accessed September 9, 2013, http://www.nhpco.org/sites/default/files/public/regulatory/ Bereavement_tip_sheet.pdf.

pice patients. In many cases, hospice workers accomplish bereavement services as they conduct their normal daily activities. Hulbert explains:

> Hospice (what foresight it now seemed to have gotten those signatures) promptly dispatched an oxygen machine, which exhaled noisily in the corner while my mother inhaled until she could once again hold her own. By the next day, with the delivery of a hospital bed placed by the windows not far from my parents' bed, we had left our rural retreat far in the past. Our new nurse, Paula, took to lingering when she came for her twice-weekly visits, plainly happy to spend time with someone so open to talking about what her patients rarely wanted to discuss death.[115]

Medicare requires hospice programs to provide support services and counseling to all family members for up to one year after the death of hospice patients, generally

---

[115] Ann Hulbert, "To Accept What Cannot Be Helped," *American Scholar* 80, no. 1 (Winter 2011): 5-6.

offering scheduled mailings of letters or notices about meetings or groups, telephone support, and literature on grief.[116] In many hospices, the bereavement coordinators are hospice spiritual counselors or social workers.

Bereavement coordinators work with other members of the interdisciplinary teams to assess families' risk factors and support needs. Coordinators then develop bereavement plans of care, which address these needs and take into account the families' and caregivers' social, religious, and cultural values and beliefs. The plan also identifies risk factors and processes for identifying complicated grief and making referrals, if needed. The goal of every bereavement care plan is to help families cope with the impending and actual death of their loved ones.

Commonly Offered Hospice Bereavement Services

Vacha-Haase also confirms that bereavement services play an important role for family members in resolving grief, reducing the possibility of complicated grief reactions, and combating the negative health consequences of loss.[117] The following list includes some of the most commonly offered bereavement support services: (1) attendance at funerals or

---

[116] Vacha-Haase, 222.
[117] Ibid.

viewings, if possible; (2) on-going contact with the bereaved family members; (3) time-limited bereavement support groups (usually six or eight meetings); (4) time-limited bereavement support groups for targeted populations, such as children, those with AIDS, bereaved men, or parents whose children have died; (5) referral to community support groups; (6) educational programs and information on the grief process, including anticipatory grief; (7) memorial services; and (8) individual bereavement counseling.

Therefore, hospice bereavement services and counseling bring invaluable assistance for family members resolving grief. They reduce the possibility of complicated grief reactions and combat the negative health consequences of loss as families cope with the loss of their loved one.

Staff Grief and Stress Management: Caring for the Caregiver

As anyone involved with palliative care can attest, the rewards are great, but so are the stresses. Hospice chaplains must be aware of factors unique to hospice work that contribute to professional stress, signs and symptoms of unrelieved stress, methods of coping with stress, and ways hospice interdisciplinary teams can help reduce the impact of stressors.

Stressful Factors Unique to Hospice Work
and Strategies for Managing Them

White identifies several stressful factors unique to
hospice work,[118] including the nature of the patients, the
nature of successful care, the redefinition of service roles,
greater responsibility in decision making, controversy over
hospice care, financial instability and limited funds, and
politics and personalities.

The nature of the patient. Continued work with dying
patients and their families means hospice caregivers and
especially chaplains are constantly experiencing all phases
of the grief process: anticipatory grief for their patients who
are nearing death; grief and mourning for patients who
have recently died; and accumulated grief over time for all
patients who have expired under their care. In few other
work settings, are caregivers constantly and simultaneously
experiencing all of these stages of grief. Acknowledging
the toll that constant grieving and mourning can take on
us as chaplains and hospice workers as well as recognizing
the ability to manage our almost continuous grief is critical to our continued success in palliative care as hospice
chaplains.

---

[118] White, 291-338.

The nature of successful care. Health care workers are trained to evaluate success as cure, but in palliative care, successful treatment involves symptom control and preserving the patient's dignity and sense of meaning in life. Social workers and spiritual counselors/hospice chaplains are trained to work with people in all phases of life. In few other settings does their client lists consist only of dying patients and grieving family members. While social, emotional, and spiritual interventions can assist patients/family members, no amount of intervention will alter the basic fact that someone is dying. The entire interdisciplinary team is constantly challenged to redefine successful care.

The redefinition of service roles. Members of the hospice interdisciplinary team are frequently called on to perform roles for which they have received little or no professional training. During their interactions with patients, social workers and chaplains may be called upon to perform basic nursing functions such as helping the patient to the bathroom, feeding, or repositioning. In their hospice work, nurses discover quickly they need to know much more than they were taught in nursing school about death and dying, communication, individual and family counseling, and Medicare/Medicaid requirements. Physicians learn they need more information about pain and symptom management, communication, and family dynamics

Frequent expectations that all interdisciplinary team members will work outside of the traditional roles for which they were professionally trained can be a primary source of stress for hospice workers that palliative care chaplains should be watching.

Greater responsibility in decision making. All members of the hospice team, especially those involved with home care, discover they have greater responsibility for decision-making in palliative care than in almost any other component of the health care system. If problems arise during home care visits, all team members, including home health aides, nurses, chaplains, and social workers, are sometimes required to make decisions on their own and take personal responsibility for those decisions. While greater responsibility for decision-making can be a great source of professional pride and growth, it can also be a source of significant stress. The isolation of home care workers also contributes to the stress of making good patient care decisions.

Controversy over hospice care. Excellent patient care and continued education of the professional and lay communities have led to greater acceptance of hospice. However, continued misunderstanding and controversy about hospice care creates added stress for team members. The rapid growth of different types of hospice programs—with varying capacities to deliver services—has contributed to disagreements among the hospice community about what constitutes hospice care. The rapid increase in privately owned, for-profit hospice programs has also generated controversy. The lack of definition and licensure requirements for hospice programs also contribute to uncertainty about what a hospice program is and what it is not.

As our society struggles with ethical issues related to terminal care, hospice workers discover that the community expects them to function as experts on ethical questions in which our entire culture wrestles. This continued controversy produces a great deal of stress for hospice workers.

Financial instability and limited funds. Some hospice programs, whether large or small, experience continued difficulties with ongoing funding. Since the basic criteria for hospice care is need for terminal care rather than the ability to pay, all hospice programs struggle with ethical questions about how to meet the growing need for hospice services, particularly among patient populations whose diseases may be viewed as more chronic than terminal, and who have tremendous social needs such as people with certain pulmonary diseases, Alzheimer's, and AIDS.

The over-85 group is one of the fastest growing populations in our western culture, and many of these have been widowed. Some have no living children or their children live thousands of miles away. Trying to meet the needs of so many patients is a continuing source of stress for many hospice professionals.

Politics and personalities. As hospice definitions continue to develop, battles over what palliative care means and what makes up hospice care will continue. In some regions, an us-versus-them attitude exists as hospice team members contemplate the incorporation or exclusion of palliative care services into the traditional health care delivery system of hospitals, nursing homes, and home health care agencies. This controversy and stress will continue as federal and state governments attempt to recreate our health care delivery system under the Affordable Health Care Act (Obama Care). All of these things produce additional professional stress as hospice workers and chaplains focus on patient care.

Scholars state the problem, "Caregivers of hospice patients provide a significant amount of care to the patient, and suffer from higher levels of stress, depression, anxiety, and physical ailments."[119] Chaplains have their own comfort levels of stress. A stress level that seems exhilarating

---

[119] Jessica Empeño, Natasha T.J. Raming, Scott A. Irwin, Richard A. Nelesen, and Linda S. Lloyd, "The Impact of Additional Support Services on Caregivers of Hospice Patients and Hospice Social Workers," *Omega: Journal of Death and Dying* 67, no. 1/2 (February 2013): 54.

and conducive to good work to one member of the inter-disciplinary team may be very frightening and overwhelming to another. Each caregiver comes to hospice work with their own vulnerabilities to stress, their own genetic makeup, and their own developmental history. Chaplains' coping abilities with stress at work and home may change over time as they experience additional stress in one or more areas of their lives. When illness hits, a level of stress that was comfortable may seem suddenly overwhelming. Dearmond reports that there is a correlation between effective self-care strategies and lower levels of burnout and compassion fatigue, as well as higher levels of compassion satisfaction.[120]

Each chaplain manages stress in different ways, some of which may not be very productive. White, in agreement with other experts on stress management, points out the following effective strategies for managing stress in caregivers' hospice work and lives:[121] know themselves, identify the stressors in their lives, set limits, listen to early warning signs, express themselves, recognize their own physical needs, recognize their own social and emotional needs, recognize their own spiritual needs, develop boundaries between their

---

[120] Dearmond, 281.
[121] White, 291-338.

personal and professional lives, avoid the super-person syndrome, develop time-alone activities, take time out, enjoy themselves, and moving on from hospice work.

Know yourself. All of us have differing abilities to cope with stress. Chaplains need to know themselves well enough to recognize the levels of stress they find satisfying and recognize when their stress levels begin to rise above a comfortable level and overwhelm them. We also need to accept ourselves as we really are. Not being able to cope with the same amount of stress as a co-worker does not mean we are inferior or lacking value as a hospice worker. One of the most important lessons in life is learning to accept ourselves. Chaplains, as well as other team members, need to let go of the desire to be someone or something we are not.

Identify the stressors in your life. Take time to recognize and label the stressors in your life as a chaplain and hospice worker and then prioritize them. If lack of clarity in your job description is producing stress, ask for clarification. If uncertainty about an aspect of your job as a spiritual counselor is creating stress, ask for help and additional training. If personal stressors are adding to professional stress, discuss the situation with your supervisor. A temporary reduction in work responsibilities might need to be arranged while you cope with a family crisis. Ask family members for more help with responsibilities at home.

Set limits. Every chaplain needs to recognize the limits of our knowledge and expertise and learn to say, "I do not know." Each of us also needs to understand the limits of our physical and emotional stamina. We have to learn when to say no to requests to take on additional responsibilities at work, at church, at home, or in civic groups.

Clarifying responsibilities in all areas of our lives and deciding on priorities is an important step in stress management. For some, family receives first priority. For others, work or church activities receive top billing. Although there are times when we need to give more of our attention to lower priority areas, continuing to devote ourselves to lower priorities leads to growing dissatisfaction and multiplied stress. We must live our lives according to our values and beliefs. We have to set limits.

Listen to early warning signs. Early warning signs tell chaplains that we are exceeding our ability to cope with stressors in our lives. These warning signs show us that we need to adjust or make some changes. White emphasizes that early warning signs are physical, emotional, relational, and behavioral.

Physical: fatigue and chronic exhaustion; sleep disturbances; muscular pain; nervous tics; and increased health problems such as headaches, colds, ulcers, etc.

Emotional: depression; loss of emotional control; feeling trapped; feelings of paranoia and/or martyrdom; inability to concentrate and increased day dreaming; preoccupation with our own death; guilt; feelings of worthlessness; irritability; constant feelings of not being valued or respected, boredom; cynicism; feelings of constant frustration; extreme mood changes.

Relational: isolation or over-dependence on co-workers; increased isolation from patients; increased anger at patients, co-workers, and supervisors; increased problems with martial or other interpersonal relationships; hypercriticism of program and/or co-workers, friends, and family members.

Behavioral: sick humor, particularly aimed at our patients; over- or under-eating; teeth grinding; increased use of alcohol, caffeine, tobacco, prescribed and/or illicit drugs; risky behavior, including speeding and not wearing seatbelts.

Express yourself. The ability to share emotions is critical for chaplains not only in hospice work, but also in the maintenance of any close interpersonal relationship. Talking about what bothers us can help release feelings and reduce stress. We can find solace in a supportive listener who accepts what we feel without blaming or judging. As we voice our feelings of grief, anxiety, overload, disappointment, guilt, anger, shame, love, concern, and affection, we are able to resolve the accumulated grief and stress that are part of the territory of hospice chaplaincy work.

We must also learn to speak up and ask for help for ourselves and others when needed. No one, not even the best supervisor, co-worker, family member, or friend, can read our minds. We must speak up for ourselves and get help with stress management. An organization may not be able to respond to all of our needs, but compromise is usually possible.

Recognize your own physical needs. Exercise, good nutrition, and adequate sleep contribute greatly to our ability to cope with stress. We need to remember to take walks and regular work breaks. Take time out for meals, regardless of how busy you are. One of the responsibilities of the hospice program is to ensure a healthy environment for all hospice workers. If adequate time for breaks and meals is not provided, speak up.

In the midst of caring for others, we may forget our own needs for physical comfort through touching, stroking, hugging, and other physical contact which relieves stress.

Recognize your own social and emotional needs. Although chaplains often talk to our patients/families about their social and emotional needs, we sometimes forget about our own. Responding to our emotional and social needs is an important strategy for managing stress. In his discussion of stress management techniques, White notes our long-range effectiveness in hospice may depend more on our ability to nurture ourselves emotionally outside work than on the knowledge and skills we bring to palliative care. While our own social and emotional sources of support can include our co-workers, they should also include people who are not associated with hospice care.

Recognize your own spiritual needs. Working with the dying creates an atmosphere in which hospice chaplains and others working in hospice care inevitably ask our own questions about the value and meaning of our lives. Once again, we need to remember working with the dying means working on ourselves. Working with dying patients and their families sometimes results in spiritual crises that are normal and to be expected. On occasion, we may question all of our spiritual and religious beliefs and values. This questioning can be very unsettling for most chaplains, but the process leads to immense growth as we allow God's presence working through us to impact the lives of so many we encounter. Sometimes, as a result of what we learn from our dying patients, our religious beliefs change, expand, and grow. In other words, God continues to mature us, even as chaplains, into more effective vessels that hold His glory.

While belief systems vary widely among hospice staff, most hospice workers say their religious beliefs are an important resource in managing their work stress. As hospice chaplains, we must recognize our spiritual needs and nurture ourselves spiritually in whatever ways we find most helpful.

Develop boundaries between your personal and professional lives. All of us need to maintain some balance between our work and personal lives. This is very difficult for many chaplains because we develop relationships with those we minister to so God's presence can impact their lives. Because working with the dying is intense and consumes a great deal of emotional energy, balancing our lives as ministers is particularly important.

Allowing our work life to consume all of our time and energy contributes to excessive stress and an unbalanced life. If we use up all of our "emotional relating" energy with our patients and their families, we have none left for our own family members and friends. While chaplains can expect some amount of understanding on the part of our spouses and/or children and friends, we cannot expect to to always come in second in our lives. Nor can we expect them to listen to all of our horror stories and work-related grief. Our homes need to be a respite from, rather than a continuation of, our work life.

Chaplains can maintain balance in our lives by making sure we develop social networks outside hospice so we can truly get away from it all. When we see our co-workers as our only friends, and when all of our socializing needs are met by co-workers or patients and their families, we can quickly lose perspective and begin to believe nothing else matters except hospice work.

We need to develop social supports among those who share similar interests and hobbies. By doing so, we revitalize ourselves and nurture our own lives, which increases our ability to nurture our patients and freely let God's presence work in their lives.

Avoid the super-person syndrome. Hospice workers are frequently tempted to become "super-persons," whether they serve as nurses, social workers, home health aides, chaplains, volunteer coordinators, secretaries, or physicians. Because our patient's needs are so great and resources are so limited, each of us is tempted to spend longer and longer hours at work trying to accomplish more and more.

Soon, even experienced chaplains can begin to believe that our patients, their family members, and the hospice program itself could not possibly get along without our presence. We begin to think we have become indispensable. We think that only we can do the job right. When we have a difficult time leaving at the end of the day, delegating tasks, relinquishing our patients to the on-call staff, or using vacation days, we need to stop and analyze our situation. Have we developed a super-person mentality? Is our over-involvement with hospice work actually reducing our effectiveness and placing a barrier between God's presence and the very people we hope to impact?

Develop time-alone activities. Each chaplain needs to remember to set aside time for ourselves and engage in activities that bring us pleasure and allow us to escape from all the roles we fill: worker, parent, spouse, and friend.

Take time out. Hospice chaplains spend a significant part of our lives at work. We need to remember to take time out during the work day to nurture ourselves by going for a walk around the block or spending a few minutes relaxing in some activity that we enjoy. This reduces stress and allows a chaplain to become more effective in allowing God's presence to flow through us to make a bigger difference in patients and their families' lives. We must use vacation days, personal leave days, and compensatory time off to refresh ourselves physically, emotionally, and spiritually so we can be at our best to help those we serve.

Enjoy yourself. Most of us take ourselves too seriously. The nature of hospice work tends to reinforce our seriousness. Make time to be silly and play. Celebrate birthdays and Ground Hog Day or wear a green wig to work on St. Patrick's Day. Blow bubbles and remember to laugh. This is our life and it will not last forever. Working at hospice and listening to our dying patients reminds us, as no other work situation can, that quality of life and enjoying the blessings of the moment truly make our lives worth living. We must enjoy the journey God has placed us on, and remember to laugh with ourselves, our co-workers, our family, and our patients and their families.

Move on. There are times when each of us recognizes that we are ready to move on to new challenges and experiences. Moving on from hospice can be a particularly difficult decision because we tend to think of hospice as a very special type of work that very few people are able to handle or perform well because of the stress.

Hospice care has the special mystique of being a radical movement that forced change in an existing and powerful system—a change brought about by the hard work of charismatic leaders and their followers who devoted much of their lives to answering a call to improve the care of the dying and to further this hospice care movement.

Too frequently, those who decide to move on from hospice do so with a profound sense of guilt. We wonder if our decision to leave means we are not a "hospice person."

Some ponder if leaving means we are weak and just cannot take it. Are we being selfish? Will our co-workers think we are abandoning them and the special hospice cause? Instead of accepting ourselves as we are and respecting our own needs for growth in other situations, we heap guilt on ourselves.

Once again we need to remember what we learn from working with the dying. Just as we encourage the dying to let go when the time is right, so we need to let go and move on when the time is right. Just as we encourage family members to tell their loved ones it is okay to let go, so we need to let go of our co-workers when the time comes.

We also need to recognize our own need to grieve. When we move on from hospice work, or from any situation in which we have invested ourselves, our caring, and our love, we need to recognize our own grieving process and that of our co-workers. We need to take time to say our good-byes and give ourselves permission to leave.

When our co-workers decide to move on to another position in hospice, or to an entirely different type of work, we need to engage in the rituals of leaving by recognizing the contributions they have made to hospice, saying our good-byes, and letting them go in peace and with Godspeed.

So as hospice chaplains manage their stress effectively, God's manifest presence will continue shining through them making the maximum kingdom impact on the patients, families, and other caregivers entrusted to their charge.

CONCLUSION

This work explored the world of hospice by first examining hospice movement history, hospice philosophy and concepts of care, hospice program models, and hospice interdisciplinary teams to develop a better understanding of what is involved as patients and caregivers interact in the palliative care environment. Section two focused on hospice spiritual care by discussing psychosocial and spiritual aspects of pain, spiritual assessments and spiritual care plans, role of the spiritual care staff, and staff grief and stress management.

The world of hospice is a unique culture, and performing spiritual care in it can be demanding. Hospice chaplains face unusual challenges and ways of adapting to those trials that set them apart. They are a much needed and sometimes under-appreciated element of this movement. Yet, in many ways, the world of hospice could not function without them. Each has exclusive roles which bring great responsibilities as they minister to patients, families, and other staff in this caring profession.

DR. DOUGLAS G. SULLIVAN

As hospice chaplains are present, allowing God's manifest glory to shine through them while providing listening ears as spiritual counselors, they provide answers many times as the struggle with the crisis of death occurs. They have priceless opportunities to minister not only to dying patients, but to their families, caregivers, and other staff as well.

People must remember that chaplains can only share what they have first experienced for themselves. To truly make a difference and to allow God's presence to flow through them, chaplains first must be healthy, balanced, and full of God's Holy Spirit so this precious resource can minister through them and change the lives of those they care for. These caregivers are ordinary people doing extraordinary jobs, often under very difficult circumstances. Hospice providers and chaplains are regular people with everyday problems of their own.

Chaplains offer comfort, kindness, and care to the dying in their communities in their greatest hours of need. The emotional, spiritual, and practical helps hospice chaplains provide through the ministry of presence can make all the difference in the world for their neighbors. Hospice chaplains are ordinary people inspired by extraordinary purpose, allowing God's manifest presence to change people's lives through palliative care.

BIBLIOGRAPHY

Hospice Related Literature

Adams, Jane P., Mary Jane Hershatter, and Derry Ann Moritz. "Accumulated Loss Phenomenon Among Hospice Caregivers." *The American Journal of Hospice and Palliative Care* 8, no. 3 (May/June 1991): 29-37.

Albrecht, Jennifer S., Ann L. Gruber-Baldini, Erik K. Fromme, Jessina C. McGregor, David S. H. Lee, and Jon P. Furuno. "Quality of Hospice Care for Individuals with Dementia." *Journal of the American Geriatrics Society* 61, no. 7 (July 2013): 1060-1065.

Amenta, Madalon O'Rawe, and Nancy L. Bohnet. *Nursing Care of the Terminally Ill.* Boston: Little Brown and Company, 1986.

"An Explanation of Palliative Care." National Hospice and Palliative Care Organization. Accessed March 20, 2015. http://www.nhpco.org/palliative-care-0.

"Appendix M, Guidance to Surveyors – Hospice," Department of Health and Human Services, Centers for Medicare and Medicaid Services, in State Operations Provider Certification, CMS.gov, Accessed May 18, 2014, http://www.cms.gov/Regulations-and-Guidance/Guidance/Manuals/downloads/som107ap_m_hospice.pdf.

Armstrong-Daily, Ann, and Sarah Zarboc Goltzer. *Hospice Care for Children.* New York: Oxford University Press, 2009.

Aroskar, Mila A. "Anatomy of an Ethical Dilemma: The Theory." *American Journal of Nursing* 80, no. 4 (April 1980): 658-660.

———. "Ethical and Legal Issues in the Care of the Terminally Ill." *Hospice Education Program for Nurses.* U.S. Department of Health and Human Services. DHHS Publication No. HRA 81-27, 1981.

Baldwin, Moyra A., and Jan Woodhouse, eds. *Key Concepts in Palliative Care.* London: SAGE Publications, Ltd., 2011.

Berman, Jeffrey. *Dying to Teach: A Memoir of Love, Loss, and Learning.* Albany, NY: State University of New York Press, 2007.

Brown, Edwina A., E. Joanna Chambers, and Celia Eggeling. *End of Life Care in Nephrology: From Advanced Disease to Bereavement.* Oxford: Oxford University Press, 2007.

Burns, Nancy, Kim Carney, and Bob Brobst. "Hospice: A Design for Home Care for the Terminally Ill." *Holistic Nursing Practice* 3, no. 2 (February 1989): 65-76.

Cassileth, Barrie R. "Methodologic Issues in Palliative Care Psychosocial Research." *Journal of Palliative Care* 5, no. 4 (December 1989): 5-11.

Cerminara, Kathy L. "Hospice and Health Care Reform: Improving Care at the End of Life." *Widener Law Review* 17, no. 2 (September 2011): 443-473.

Chandler, Cynthia K., Janice Miner Holden, and Cheryl A. Kolander. "Counseling for Spiritual Wellness: Theory and Practice." *Journal of Counseling and Development* 71 (November/December 1992): 168-175.

Cheston, Sharon E., and Robert J. Wicks. *Essentials for Chaplains.* Mahwah, NJ: Paulist Press, 1993.

Chow, Edward, and Joav Merrick. *Advanced Cancer: Pain and Quality of Life.* New York: Nova Science, 2010.

Conner, Stephen R. *Hospice and Palliative Care: The Essential Guide.* 2nd ed. New York: Taylor and Francis Group, 2009.

Corless, Inge B., Barbara B. Germino, and Mary Pittman, eds. *Dying, Death, and Bereavement: A Challenge for Living.* 2nd ed. New York: Springer Publishing Co., 2006.

Coward, Harold G., and Kelli I. Stajduhar, eds. *Religious Understandings of a Good Death in Hospice Palliative Care.* Albany, NY: State University of New York Press, 2012.

Davies, Pamela S., and Yvonne M. D'Arcy. *Compact Clinical Guide to Cancer Pain Management: An Evidence-based Approach for Nurses.* New York: Springer Publishing Co., 2013.

Davidson, Glen W. *Understanding Mourning: A Guide for Those Who Grieve.* Minneapolis, MN: Augsburg Publishing House, 1984.

Dearmond, Isabelle M. "The Psychological Experience of Hospice Workers during Encounters with Death." *Omega: Journal of Death & Dying* 66, no. 4 (December 2012): 281-299.

Empeño, Jessica, Natasha T. J. Raming, Scott A. Irwin, Richard A. Nelesen, and Linda S. Lloyd. "The Impact of Additional Support Services on Caregivers of Hospice Patients and Hospice Social Workers." *Omega:*

Journal of Death and Dying 67, no. 1/2 (February 2013): 53-61.

Floyd, Scott. *Crisis Counseling: A Guide for Pastors and Professionals.* Grand Rapids: Kregel Academic and Professional, 2008.

Fowlie, Midge, John Berkeley, and Ianthe Dingwall-Fordyce. "Quality of Life in Advanced Cancer: The Benefits of Asking the Patient." *Palliative Medicine* 3, no. 1 (January 1989): 55-59.

Fulton, Robert, and Julie Fulton. "A Psychosocial Aspect of Terminal Care: Anticipatory Grief." *Omega* 2 (1971): 91-99.

Groupman, Jerome. "The Grief Industry: How Much Does Crisis Counseling Help—Or Hurt?" The New Yorker. Accessed June 25, 2013. http://www.newyorker.com/magazine/2004/01/26/the-grief-industry.

Hall, Daleasha, Mary A. Shirey, and David C. Waggoner. "Improving Access and Satisfaction with Spiritual Care in the Hospice Setting." *Omega: Journal of Death & Dying* 67, no. 1/2 (February 2013): 97-107.

Hansen, James C., and Thomas T. Frantz. *Death and Grief in the Family.* Rockville, MD: Aspen Systems, 1984.

Hay, Milton W. "Principles in Building Spiritual Assessment Tools." *The American Journal of Hospice and Palliative Care* 6, no. 5 (September/October 1989): 25-31.

Herson, Jay. "Hospice Leaders Attend Innovative Futuring Forum." *Futurist* 47, no. 3 (May 2013): 60.

Hillyard, Daniel, and John Dombrink. *Dying Right: The Death with Dignity Movement.* New York: Routledge, 2002.

"HIPAA: Questions and Answers for Family Caregivers." Next Step in Care. Accessed June 25, 2013. http://www.nextstepincare.org/Caregiver_Home/HIPAA/?gclid=CJ2kj5Tmh7g

CFYYWMgod2mgA3A.

Hollingsworth, Charles. "Role Adjustments in Families after Death." *World Journal of Psychosynthesis* 10, no. 4 (1978): 13-16.

Hulbert, Ann. "To Accept What Cannot Be Helped." *American Scholar* 80, no. 1 (Winter 2011): 57-70.

Hurley, Ann, and Ladislav Volicer. *Hospice Care for Patients with Advanced Progressive Dementia.* New York: Springer Publishing Co., 1998.

"Interdisciplinary Team." National Hospice and Palliative Care Organization. Accessed September 9, 2013. http://www.nhpco.org/interdisciplinary-team.

James, Richard K., and Burl E. Gilliland. *Crisis Intervention Strategies.* 7th ed. Belmont: Brooks/Cole, Cengage Learning, 2013.

Jenkins, Hugh. "The Family and Loss: A Systems Framework." *Palliative Medicine* 3, no. 2 (April 1989): 97-104.

Jung, Carl G. "The Soul and Death." In *The Meaning of Death*, edited by H. Feifel, 3-15. New York: McGraw-Hill, 1959.

Kalish, Richard A. "The Onset of the Dying Process." *Omega* 1, no. 1 (1970): 57-69.

———. "The Effects of Death upon the Family." In *Death and Dying: Current Issues in Treatment of the Dying Person*, edited by Leonard Pearson, 79-107. Cleveland, OH: Press of Case Western Reserve University, 1969.

Kübler-Ross, Elisabeth. *On Death and Dying.* New York: Macmillian Publishing Company, 1969.

Kramer, Betty J., Melinda Kavanaugh, Amy Trentham-Dietz, Matthew Walsh, and James A. Yonker. "Complicated Grief Symptoms in Caregivers of Persons with Lung Cancer: The Role of Family Conflict, Intrapsychic Strains, and Hospice Utilization." *Omega: Journal of Death & Dying* 62, no. 3 (September 2010): 201-220.

Kramer, Kenneth Paul. *The Sacred Art of Dying: How World Religions Understand Death.* Mahwah, NJ: Paulist Press, 1988.

Lack, Sylvia A., and Robert W. Buckingham, III. *First American Hospice: Three Years of Home Care.* New Haven: Hospice, Inc., 1978.

Latimer, Elizabeth. "Ethical Challenges in Cancer Care." *Journal of Palliative Care* 8, no. 1 (Spring 1992): 65-70.

Lawton, Julia. *The Dying Process: Patients' Experiences of Palliative Care.* London: Routledge, 2000.

Lawton, M. Powell. *Focus on the End of Life: Scientific and Social Issues.* New York: Springer Publishing Co., 2001.

Levine, Stephen. *Who Dies? An Investigation of Conscious Living and Conscious Dying.* New York: Random House, Inc., 1982.

Lindemann, Erich. "Symptomatology and Management of Acute Grief." *American Journal of Psychiatry* 10 (1944): 141-148.

MacDonald, Douglas. "Hospice, Entropy, and the 1990s: Toward a Hospice World View." *The American Journal of Hospice and Palliative Care* 7, no. 4 (July/August 1990): 39-47.

———. "Hospice Social Work: A Search for Identity." *Health and Social Work* 16, no. 4 (November 1991): 274-280.

———. "The Hospice World View: Healing vs. Recovery." *The American Journal of Hospice and Palliative Care* 7, no. 5 (September/October 1990): 40-45.

McCormick, Richard. *How Brave a New World*. New York: Doubleday, 1981.

"Medicare Hospice Conditions of Participation Bereavement." National Hospice and Palliative Care Organization. Accessed September 9, 2013. http://www.nhpco.org/sites/default/files/public/regulatory/Bereavement_tip_sheet.pdf.

"Medicare Hospice Conditions of Participation Spiritual Caregiver." National Hospice and Palliative Care Organization. Accessed September 9, 2013. http://www.nhpco.org/sites/default/files/public/regulatory/Spiritual_tip_sheet.pdf.

Miller, James E., with Susan C. Cutshall. *The Art of Being a Healing Presence: A Guide for Those in Caring Relationships*. Ft. Wayne, IN: Willowgreen Publishing, 2001.

Miller, Judy. "Signs and Symptoms of Approaching Death." Amarillo, TX: St. Anthony's Hospice, 1986.

Minuchin, Salvador. *Families and Family Therapy.* London: Tavistock Publications, 1974.

National Hospice Organization (NHO). *Standards of a Hospice Program of Care.* Arlington, VA: NHO, 1993.

National Hospice and Palliative Care Organization (NHPCO). *Standards of Practice for Hospice Programs (2010).* Arlington, VA: NHPCO, 2010.

Noe, Kelly, Pamela Smith, and Mustafa Younis. "Calls for Reform to the U.S. Hospice System." *Ageing International* 37, no. 2 (June 2012): 228-237.

O'Shaughnessy, Charles Owen. *To Comfort the Dying: A Guide to Hospice Care.* Grants Pass, OR: Lovejoy Hospice, 1996.

Parkes, Colin. M. "Effects of Bereavement on Physical and Mental Health: A Study of the Medical Records of Widows." *British Medical Journal* 2 (1964): 274-279.

Pellegrino, Edmund D. "The Metamorphosis of Medical Ethics." *The Journal of the American Medical Association* 269, no. 9 (March 1993): 1158-1162.

Putnam, Constance E. *Hospice or Hemlock? Searching for Heroic Compassion.* Westport, CT: Praeger Publishers, 2002.

Quig, Lois. "The Role of the Hospice Social Worker." *American Journal of Hospice and Palliative Care* (July/ August 1989): 22-23.

Quinlan-Colwell, Ann. *Compact Clinical Guide to Geriatric Pain Management: An Evidence-based Approach for Nurses.* New York: Springer Publishing Co., 2012.

Rae-Grant, Quentin. "The Hazards of Team Work." *American Journal of Orthopsychiatry*38, no. 1 (January 1968): 4-8.

Rando, Therese A. "Concepts of Death, Dying, Grief and Loss." *Hospice Education Program for Nurses.* U.S. Department of Health and Human Services. DHHS Publication No. HRA 81-27, 1981.

Satir, Virginia. *The New Peoplemaking.* Mountain View, CA: Science and Behavior Books, 1988.

Saunders, Dame Cicely. *The Management of Terminal Disease.* London: Edward Arnold, Ltd., 1978.

———. "Spiritual Pain." *Journal of Palliative Care* 4, no. 3 (September 1988): 29-32.

———. "The Moment of Truth: Care of the Dying Patient." In *Death and Dying: Current Issues in Treatment of the Dying Person,* edited by Leonard Pearson, 48-78.

Cleveland, OH: Press of Case Western Reserve University, 1969.

Saunders, Cicely M., and David Clark. *Cicely Saunders: Founder of the Hospice Movement: Selected Letters 1959-1999.* Oxford: Oxford University Press, 2002.

Saunders, Cicely M., Dorothy H. Summers, and Neville E. Teller, eds. *Hospice: The Living Idea.* London: Edward Arnold, Ltd., 1981.

Strickland, Jennifer M. *Palliative Pharmacy Care.* Bethesda, MD: American Society of Health- System Pharmacists, 2009.

"Standards of Practice for Hospice Programs (2010)." National Hospice and Palliative Care Organization (NHPCO). Accessed May 9, 2014. http://www.nhpco.org/standards.

Stoddard, Sandol. *The Hospice Movement: A Better Way of Caring for the Dying.* New York: Random House, Inc., 1978.

Teno, Joan M., Pedro L. Gozalo, Ian C. Lee, Sylvia Kuo, Carol Spence, Stephen R. Connor, and David J. Casarett. "Does Hospice Improve Quality of Care for Persons Dying from Dementia?" *Journal of The American Geriatrics Society* 59, no. 8 (August 2011): 1531-1536.

"Traumatic Loss Coalitions for Youth Program-The Tasks of Grieving." Rutgers University Behavioral HealthCare Behavioral Research and Training Institute. Accessed June 29, 2013. http://ubhc.rutgers.edu/brti/tlc/guide lines/TasksOfGrieving.

Vacha-Haase, Tammi. "The 'We Care' Program for Long-Term Care: Providing Family Members with Support Following the Death of a Loved One." *Omega: Journal of Death & Dying* 67, no. 1/2 (February 2013): 221-226.

Vandergrift, Alison. "Use of Complementary Therapies in Hospice and Palliative Care." *Omega: Journal of Death & Dying* 67, no. 1/2 (February 2013): 227-232.

Wald, Florence S. "Hospice Care Concepts," Hospice Education Program for Nurses. U.S. Department of Health and Human Services. DHHS Publication No. HRA 81-27, 1981.

Wald, Florence S., Zelda Foster, and Henry J. Wald, "The Hospice Movement as a Health Care Reform," *American Journal of Nursing* 79, no. 10 (October 1979): 173-178.

Wanzer, Sidney. "The Physicians Responsibility Toward Hopelessly Ill Patients: A Second Look." *The New*

England Journal of Medicine 320 (March 30, 1989): 844-849.

Weissman, Avery D., and Thomas P. Hackett. "Predilections to Death." *Psychosomatic Medicine.* Vol. 23. 1961.

Wellisch, David.K. "An Evaluation of the Psycho-social Problems of the Homebound Cancer Patient." *Journal of Psychosocial Oncology,* 7, no. 1-2 (1989): 55-76.

White, William L. "Managing Personal and Organizational Stress in the Care of the Dying." *Hospice Education Program for Nurses.* U.S. Department of Health and Human Services. DHHS Publication No. HRA 81-27, 1981.

Wolfelt, Alan D. *A Child's View of Grief: A Guide for Parents, Teachers, and Counselors.* Ft. Collins, CO: Companion Press, 2004.

———. "Toward an Understanding of Complicated Grief: A Comprehensive Overview." *The American Journal of Hospice and Palliative Care* 8, no. 2 (March/April 1991): 28-30.

Worden, William J. "Bereavement." In *Seminars in Oncology* 12, no. 4 (December 1985): 472-475.

———. *Grief Counseling and Grief Therapy.* 4th ed. New York: Springer Publishing Company, 2009.

Worden, William J., and James R. Monahan. "Caring for Bereaved Parents." In *Hospice Care for Children,* 3rd ed., edited by Ann Armstrong-Daily and Sarah Zarboc Goltzer, 181-200. New York: Oxford University Press, 2008.

Wright, H. Norman. *Crisis and Trauma Counseling: What to Do and Say When It Matters Most.* Ventura: Regal Books from Gospel Light, 2011.

Young-Brockopp, Dorothy. "Statements of Hope of the Terminally Ill: Cancer Patients' Perception of Their Psychosocial Needs." *Oncology Nursing Forum* 9, no. 4 (1982): 31-35.

Missional/Spiritual Leadership Related Literature

Barton, Ruth Haley. *Strengthening the Soul of Your Leadership.* Downers Grove, IL: InterVarsity, 2008.

Bennis, Warren. *On Becoming a Leader.* New York: Basic Books, 2003.

Blanchard, Ken, and Phil Hodges. *Lead Like Jesus: Lessons from the Greatest Leadership Role Model of All Time.* Nashville: Thomas Nelson, 2008.

Brandt, R. L. *Gifts for the Marketplace.* Tulsa, OK: Christian Publishing Services, Inc., 1989.

Clinton, J. Robert. *The Making of a Leader: Recognizing the Lessons and Stages of Leadership Development.* Colorado Springs: NavPress, 1988.

Creps, Earl. *Off-Road Disciplines: Spiritual Adventures of Missional Leaders.* San Francisco: Jossey-Bass/ Leadership Network, 2006.

———. *Reverse Mentoring: How Young Leaders Can Transform the Church and Why We Should Let Them.* San Francisco: Jossey-Bass, 2008.

Demarest, Bruce. *Seasons of the Soul: Stages of Spiritual Development.* Downers Grove, IL: InterVarsity Press, 2009.

DePree, Max. *Leading without Power: Finding Hope in Serving Community.* San Francisco: Jossey-Bass, 1997.

Drane, John. *After McDonaldization: Mission, Ministry and Christian Discipleship in an Age of Uncertainty.* Grand Rapids: Baker, 2008.

Greenleaf, Robert K. *Servant Leadership: A Journey into the Life of Legitimate Power and Greatness.* 25th anniversary ed. Mahwah, NJ: Paulist Press, 2002.

Hesselgrave, David. *Communicating Christ Cross-Culturally: An Introduction to Missionary Communication.* 2nd ed. Grand Rapids: Zondervan, 1991.

Holm, Neil. "Practising the Ministry of Presence in Chaplaincy." *Journal of Christian Education* 52, no. 3 (December 2009): 29-42.

———. "Toward a Theology of the Ministry of Presence in Chaplaincy." *Journal of Christian Education* 52, no. 1 (May 2009): 7-22.

Joiner, Reggie, Lane Jones, and Andy Stanley. *The 7 Practices of Effective Ministry.* Sisters, OR: Multnomah, 2004.

Matthews, Warren. *World Religions.* 7th ed. Belmont CA: Wadsworth, 2013.

Mancini, Will. *Church Unique: How Missional Leaders Cast Vision, Capture Culture, and Create Movement.* 1st ed. San Francisco: Jossey-Bass, 2008.

MacDonald, Gordon. *Who Stole My Church: What to Do When the Church You Love Tries to Enter the 21st Century.* Reprint ed. Nashville: Thomas Nelson, 2010.

———. *Going Deep: Becoming a Person of Influence.* Nashville: Thomas Nelson, 2011.

Murrow, David. *Why Men Hate Going to Church.* Nashville: Thomas Nelson, 2011.

Nouwen, Henri. *In the Name of Jesus: Reflections on Christian Leadership.* New York: Crossroad, 1989.

Paget, Naomi K., and Janet R. McCormack. *The Work of the Chaplain*. Valley Forge, PA: Judson Press, 2006.

Smith, Huston. *The World Religions*. New York: Harper Collins, 2009.

Stetzer, Ed, and Philip Nation. *Compelled: Living the Mission of God*. Birmingham, AL: New Hope Publishers, 2012.

Sweet, Leonard. *Summoned to Lead*. Grand Rapids: Zondervan, 2004.

U.S. Department of the Air Force. *Professional Development Guide*. AF Pamphlet 36-2241. Washington, DC: Government Printing Office, 2011.

Veith, Gene Edward. *God at Work: Your Christian Vocation in All of Life*. Wheaton, IL: Crossway Books, 2002.

Viola, Frank. *Reimagining Church: Pursuing the Dream of Organic Christianity*. Colorado Springs: David C. Cook, 2008.

Doug Sullivan, an insightful and powerful teacher of God's Word, has served as a lead pastor, college professor, chaplain, and counselor for over thirty years. Dr. Sullivan is a retired USAF officer who continues to serve as a Lieutenant Colonel in the Texas Civil Defense, where he oversees all chaplain and benevolence ministries. He is also an adjunct professor at the Waxahachie Campus of Navarro College where he teaches religion, philosophy, and orientation. Doug is the emergency services chaplain for the Maypearl Fire Department, while also providing hospice and bereavement services to patients, families, and caregivers in the South Dallas area as a spiritual counselor for Bristol Hospice Pathways.

Chaplain Sullivan completed his doctoral studies in pastoral care and counseling at Evangel University in Springfield, Missouri. Doug received his Master of Divinity in practical theology from Regent University School of Divinity in Virginia Beach, Virginia. He also has completed all course work for his MS in counseling and human development from Troy State University in Troy, Alabama.

Doug's many hobbies include gardening, landscaping, hunting, fishing, and restoring antique vehicles. He is married to his high school sweetheart, Debbie who teaches special needs children. They are blessed with two married children: Daniel, a Dallas Texas police officer; and Catherine, an elementary school teacher. The Sullivans also have three wonderful grandchildren, Sophia, Ty, and Emma, and they spend much of their time spoiling them on their small farm just south of Dallas, Texas.

CPSIA information can be obtained
at www.ICGtesting.com
Printed in the USA
LVHW012148071219
639780LV00004B/83/P